HEARTS
ON FIRE

HEARTS ON FIRE

THE TAO OF MEDITATION

THE BIRTH OF
QUANTUM PSYCHOLOGY

STEPHEN WOLINSKY, PH.D.

Printed in Canada

Cover and text design:
The Bramble Company, Ojai, California

Special thanks to Mary Kowit for essential and skilled efforts
in the production of this edition.

ISBN: 0-9670362-8-3
QUANTUM INSTITUTE PRESS
Telephone (831) 464-0564
FAX (831) 479-8233

THIS BOOK IS DEDICATED TO:

Bhagawan Nityananda,
who left his body in 1961, and who is my
Acarya Guru.

To my teacher
Sri Nisargadatta Maharaj,
who separated me from identification
with the "I" and who is the ultimate
deprogrammer.

ACKNOWLEDGMENTS

Swami Muktananda,
Swami Prakashananda,
Swami Pranavananda.

Carol Agneessens and
Dorothy Agneessens who
encouraged me to get this
manuscript published.
Karl Robinson, Melissa
Patterson, Larry Marrich,
Carolyn Mountain, for their love
and support. Barbara Hoon, my
original copy editor, and Susan
Briley, word processor.

Special thanks to all my
workshop participants who sat
with me for hours in my living
room teaching me the power of
love.

CONTENTS

ABOUT THE AUTHOR

STEPHEN H. WOLINSKY, PH.D., began his clinical practice in Los Angeles, California, in 1974. A Gestalt and Reichian therapist and trainer, he led workshops in Southern California. He was also trained in classical hypnosis, Psychosynthesis, Psychodrama Psychomotor, and Transactional Analysis. In 1977 he journeyed to India, where he lived for almost six years studying meditation. He moved to New Mexico in 1982 to resume a clinical practice. There he began to train therapists in Ericksonian Hypnosis, and family therapy. Dr. Wolinsky also conducted year long trainings entitled: Integrating Hypnosis with Psychotherapy, and Integrating Hypnosis with Family Therapy. Dr. Wolinsky is also the author of *Trances People Live: Healing Approaches in Quantum Psychology, Quantum Consciousness: The Guide to Experiencing Quantum Psychology, The Dark Side of the Inner Child: The Next Step, The Tao of Chaos: Essence and the Enneagram, The Way of the Human Triology, Intimate Relationships; The Beginners Guide to Quantum Psychology,* and *I Am That I Am.* He is the founder of Quantum Psychology.

Dr. Stephen Wolinsky presently resides in Capitola, California, and can be reached at (831) 464-0564 or FAX (831) 479-8233

HEARTS
ON FIRE

PROLOGUE

There were many purposes in writing this book, *Hearts on Fire*. First is motivation. My first motivation was *a heart on fire* to know the truth about who I am. My second, and even more primary drive, was my pain. It was the psycho-emotional pain which set my *heart on fire* to find a way out or through to the other side.

In the song *"Break On Through to the Other Side"* by the Doors, Jim Morrison says of his group, we were using the music to *break through."* In my case, however, the emotional pain was used to break through.

This book really chronicles the many meditations and processes that "I" explored throughout "my" journey. However, it was not until 1982 that I began teaching classes in my living room in Albuquerque, New Mexico. This book represents the edited and highlighted transcripts of these classes. This was done so that the reader hopefully could experience and "get the feel" of what it was like to sit in these *early* meditation groups. Thus, the transcripts follow a natural stream of **consciousness** rather than a formal meditation text.

When "I" began presenting ongoing classes in meditation, my purpose began to shift. "I" wanted to offer people an opportunity to experience and integrate into their own work and Western psychology, two major paths of India: Vedanta Marg and Tantric Marg. Vedanta is the path of self-enquiry which has its roots in the ancient Upanishads and the Advaita Vedanta expounded by the 8th-century philosopher-saint Shankaracharya. The purpose is to dis-identify from beliefs and thought constructs which limit awareness and create problem states. In recent times this tradition has been clearly expressed in the lives and teachings of Ramana Maharshi and my teacher, Sri Nisargadatta Maharaj.

The Tantric path described in this book is derived from the teachings of Kashmir Shaivism, which had its origins in the 8th century in the valleys of Kashmir. The *Shiva Sutras,* the original text of Kashmir Shaivism, was reportedly communicated to the sage Vasugupta in a dream.

This book is divided into various types of "self-work", with explanations and examples drawn from my experiences with students, individually and in classes. Actually, the original text became my doctoral dissertation and later was used in the birth of Quantum Psychology. In 1993, much of the material used in my book, *Quantum Consciousness: The Guide to Experiencing Quantum Psychology,* came from this original text. Several friends of mine wanted me to publish this book because they felt it conveyed a deeper level of energy along with the birth and context of *Quantum*

Psychology. Furthermore, it was more direct and followed "my" journey more closely.

The objectives of practicing these forms of "self-work" meditations are threefold:

1. To develop a witnessing **consciousness** so that there is less identification with individual **consciousness.**
2. To move beyond limitations of mind, be they "good" or "bad," "pleasant" or "unpleasant."

   In the Shiva Sutras it says: Knowledge (information) is bondage; therefore, any information you have about yourself is limiting, and identification with this information can be observed and ultimately let go of.
3. The transmutation of psycho-emotional states.

   For example, anger, joy, and fear, can be transmuted and experienced as made of their most basic substance, namely, "energy" or **consciousness.**

According to Patanjali, author of the Yoga *Sutras,* "Yoga is stilling the thoughts of the mind." The methods presented here are a *major* contrast to Patanjali's yoga psychology. Instead of trying to "control" the mind's activities, as Patanjali teaches, the approach presented here teaches us to "witness" the mind's activities, and thus accept and allow what is there to be there. I once asked my teacher, Nisargadatta Maharaj, "Since I began self-enquiry I am overwhelmed with thoughts. Am I thinking more, or witnessing more?" He answered,

"Witnessing more. Let the mind do what it likes. You stay out of it and witness." Nisargadatta taught of pure witnessing, without attempting to change the content of the mind.

The understandings that are presented throughout *Hearts on Fire* are:

1. That everything is made of "energy" or **consciousness** in different shapes or forms, whether thoughts, emotions, feelings, beliefs, or objects.
2. That everything in life comes and goes and changes-thoughts, people, feelings, etc.
3. That "you" are the unchanging presence or permanent "I" that witnesses all of the changing "I's," i.e., "I feel good", "I feel bad", "I like you", "I don't like you".

Jnana Yoga is called the path of knowledge-actually, it is a path of *unlearning*. In the movie Star Wars, Yoda, Luke Skywalker's teacher, says to him, "You must unlearn that which you have learned."

In the path of the Jnani, anything transient is discarded as "not this, not this." Only the permanent *"You"* is kept. In Kashmir Shaivism, everything is included as "and this, and this," and is seen as "energy" or **consciousness**. This approach appreciates that every seeker must follow the method which best suits his or her own personal style. In other words, all too often meditation teachers give the *same* practice or mantra to all of their students. This "one size fits all" spirituality misses two important understandings: First, everyone is different and hence needs a different individual approach. Second, not all meditations are good for *everything*. For example, there are some meditations and forms of "self-work" that are better for emotional states, some for thought processes, and some for living in the world. In this way, this book offers a menu of many approaches, so that the practitioner can pick and choose what works for them. Furthermore, it needs to be appreciated that what works now might not work later. Therefore, the reader is asked to pick and choose, and tailor-make their own path and method, discarding that which does not fit.

How then do Eastern philosophy and approaches integrate into Western psychotherapy? In schools of psychotherapy such as Psychosynthesis, a major emphasis is the development of a witness or observer. In psychosynthesis, it is the observer who observes what is cultivated and developed.

The Fourth Way, the "Neo-Sufi" approach of G.I. Gurdjieff, puts emphasis on being objective, which he calls objectivity. The path of Buddhism spends time developing witness **consciousness** and the ability to be mindful, aware and observant of ideas, thoughts, emotions, intentions, etc.

This book offers many ways to develop the pure objective state which has been prescribed and discussed as being of paramount importance in Western psychotherapy to integrate and let go of problem states and in Eastern philosophy to *trance-end* identification with the mind.

What then is pure meditation? Meditation is a practice which develops a steady stream of uninterrupted awareness. Often the metaphor of oil being poured continuously without interruption is used to describe this flow of awareness. It is not trying to create a state, but rather an observation of what is. This pure observation means no judgement (this state is bad and this one is good), evaluation (this state means *this* or *that* about me), or significance (this state is more important or spiritual than *that* state).

Unfortunately, in the West, meditation is often depicted as a Yogi, self-efforting, resisting desires, eyes closed, in a deep self-absorption removed from the world. Actually, when meditation is "grokked," the uninterrupted flow of awareness is experienced while walking, talking, eating, sleeping, experiencing life, and even while making love. Often, as will be mentioned later, the pain that occurs in daily life can be fuel that is utilized to bring one into a deeper sense of "who you are."

As most self-explorers know, neurotic behavior or self-defeating emotional patterns are caused by interruptions. More specifically, "E" means outward; therefore, E-motion means outward motion. It is this interruption in the outward motion which occurs either by self stopping self, or other stopping self, that pulls an individual off center. Psycho-spiritual paths and techniques have the goal of handling the causes of these interruptions, which are resistance to the non-experienced experience, so that a steady, uninterrupted flow of awareness can occur. Unfortunately, in most therapy, the attention is placed on the story of *why* you are experiencing pain, rather than on the YOU which is witnessing and beyond the pain: namely, the changeless YOU. Stated another way, by shifting the focus of attention to the witnessing *you*, the mind appears and disappears in **consciousness**.

After spending years in the early '70s exploring psychology and meditation, I left for India. For six years in India, and in the United States, I had the opportunity to work directly with almost 60 teachers, gurus, and saints.

Through this, the basic understanding got clarified; *Yoga means union.* Undoubtedly, what we all have been searching for in different ways and paths is union with the **SELF** or the underlying unity. Some call it the Tao, some self-realization, I often refer to it as Quantum **Consciousness**, but it still remains the underlying unity which is us all.

In India, the Sanskrit word *Sadhana* is used to describe the practice that is utilized each day in order to attain what I call this stateless state of the Non-Being Being. *Sadhana* (The Practice) most often is *not* a natural "in the world" process. However, the challenge is to become fully absorbed, aware and awake without interruption, while living in the world rather than shutting yourself off from different aspects of the world or different aspects of yourself. This can occur quite naturally while reading, writing, during intimacy, or even watching a movie. The absorption of the "I" is so complete that there is no "I"; *this is meditation* and what is called Samadhi or no me.

Often though, even after years of exploring disciplines, the mind can still pull us off.

The only job of a true teacher therefore is to give you the means or ways to work with *yourself.* The rest must be explored on your own, without the need for constant supervision in the climate and privacy of your own being.

The techniques of this book arise from two sources: first, Jnana Yoga-this path of unlearning, also translated as the Yoga of Divine Knowledge. Second, the Secret Esoteric Teaching of Kashmiri Tantric Yoga-the path of direct recognition through the utilization of each daily experience as a means to expand and explore **consciousness.** Tantric Yoga I call the Yoga of the World, since everyone starts where they are, with no higher or lower, no resistance, no goods or bads. what is always encouraged, however, is an in-depth experimentation and exploration of who you imagine you are but ultimately are not.

This book offers approaches whose origin and roots of self-realization and self-exploration have been successfully utilized for centuries.

I hope this book serves you as a useful and *practical* way of working with "yourself" so that your *heart on fire* is no longer driven by pain, but by *love.*

With love,
Your brother; Stephen
(Prologue written December 7, 1984 Madras, India)

THE
BEGINNINGS

1 / THE BEGINNINGS

As I pondered an introductory chapter, what arose was: where do we begin and end, or are the beginning and the ending the same? As we move toward working on or perfecting the mind, what would be the impact when we discover that *we are not our minds*? From a model of Western psychotherapy it can be clearly understood that in order to let go of or be free or accept oneself, the *mind* must be cleared so the *heart* can stay open with no distractions. The highest goal and purpose of Western psychotherapy is to free the individual, utilizing techniques which range from body work, to emotional release and breath, from cognitive understanding to analytical models, and hypnotic approaches. It is obvious that all schools wish to create freedom and each provides its own technology to produce that result.

Nisargadatta Maharaj used to say that "in order to let go of something, first you must know what it is." Western therapies offer us that possibility; while Eastern approaches give us the space to explore the parts of "ourselves" in a climate of objectivity. Regardless of the path of discovery we choose, the purpose is to recover the most *basic substance* from which the mind is composed, namely CONSCIOUSNESS. The thirteenth-century poet-saint Jnaneshwar Maharaj, in his *Amritanubhava,* so elegantly called CONSCIOUS-NESS "the Divine Substance." Nisargadatta Maharaj writes "to go beyond the mind, one must look past the mind and its contents." Then what will arise is the question: If I'm not my mind, then who am I?

You are beyond thoughts and constructs of yourself-namely, pure CONSCIOUSNESS. This book provides Western therapies with the context of pure awareness, as a way of viewing the mind.

The second chapter of this book deals with techniques which enable us to go beyond repression or expression to transmutation. This is the *third option.* It is often said that in order to have choice you need three options; therefore, the repress-express dichotomy only gives us two, which is not enough. Transmutation of psycho-emotional experience is the *third choice.* To practice the art of inner transmutation, we must first explore experiences, thoughts, feeling, etc. as CON-SCIOUSNESS. It is not enough to read and theorize: We must experience developing our awareness, so that we can focus and utilize experiences as fuel to enhance the understanding that everything is made of the same substance in varied forms. This therefore becomes both the means and end.

Awareness seems to develop, maintain and grow, only with the letting-go of the identification with the mind as me and seeing it as made of its most basic substance, namely, CONSCIOUSNESS. Once this is understood and experienced fully, the world becomes, as the title of Swami Muktananda's autobiography suggests, *The Play of CONSCIOUSNESS.*- Where can we go where energy or CONSCIOUSNESS is not? where can you go where you are not? Simply ask yourself, "who is it that watches and knows the thoughts, feelings, and experiences that happen to 'you'?" The answer: *"The Witness."*

Focus your attention then on the witness which always watches; this is developing witness CON-SCIOUSNESS.

This book is organized to demonstrate ways to focus your awareness, to bring you more deeply into your own "self" Focus your attention deeply as you use these methods. The practice of meditation, or focusing and developing your awareness, is like developing a new muscle. This helps us to realize that *we are already the goal of our own search.*

SELF-ENQUIRY

2 / SELF-ENQUIRY

Self-enquiry needs to be experienced as the context for the self-explorer, as well as the therapist or counselor whose task it is to free an individual from identification with unwanted behavior patterns.

Once an individual begins to appreciate that she is not her thoughts, feelings, emotions, but rather a witnessing presence, a greater clarity emerges. Some call that presence the ''witness,'' the **I AM** or the ''inner-self.'' Often, upon applying these techniques with oneself, understandings develop.

I have broken this chapter into sections that discuss several approaches to self-enquiry.

FROM WHERE DOES THAT THOUGHT ARISE?

Meditate: *When a thought arises in meditation, ask "From where does that thought arise?"*

When we continually ask ourselves, "From where does that thought arise?", we soon learn that a thought arises, and subsides, and then there is a space. Asking yourself after each thought, "From where does that thought arise?" brings us back to that space between two thoughts so that we can witness the rising and subsiding of each thought.

For example, imagine you awaken in the morning, and next to you is the person you love. A thought comes into your awareness that says, "This is far out, I really like this." Then all of a sudden your mind will think, "I like the way they look," or "I like how smart they are " or "I like the way he/she sleeps next to me," etc. Two or three days later, you wake up and look at your lover and think, "Oh, no, what am I doing with her/him?" The next thing you find yourself thinking, "I really would like to go out with somebody else," or "maybe I should get a divorce," or "what a mistake, I am wasting my time."

An even more common experience is to wake up in the morning feeling very good; a thought goes by your awareness called "I feel good," and the witness identifies with that thought. Your mind will then start coming up with reasons why you feel good: "I feel good because I got a lot of sleep"; "I feel good because I didn't sleep very much"; "I feel good because I meditated this morning"; "I feel good because I had a lot for dinner"; "I feel good because I didn't have a lot for dinner." Around noon, a thought will go by which says, "I'm tired," and if the witness identifies with that thought, you may say, "I'm tired and why do I have to go to work? It's such a drag, I knew I slept too much or I didn't sleep enough," or whatever the sequence of events you might be experiencing. What happens is, a thought arises and subsides, and there's a space. This is the way thoughts occur-they arise, and subside, and there's space.

The purpose of the first meditation is to bring you back into *the space between two thoughts*. Understand that anything you identify with will limit you. For example, "I like blue shirts, I like red shirts. I like tall women, I like short women," whatever it may be. Whatever you believe will limit you. Or you could say that anything you identify with, or feel attached to, yields a limiting experience.

The phrase "not being attached to" is the key. A thought goes by called "I feel good," or "I feel bad, I wish I were there, I'm here, I wish I weren't here." Anything you identify yourself with as "I" will limit you. *The nature of the mind is to always change its mind;* that's why one minute you like your job, the next you don't. One minute you like your relationship, the next you don't. One day you're really happy with the course of your life; the next day you're not. If you fall in love today, tomorrow you won't like the person so much. Therefore, you can't depend on the thoughts contained within the mind.

The only thing you can depend on is *that which is witnessing the mind.* Look into your experience and ask yourself, "Who is it that is always witnessing my mind-who is it that is always there watching me?" Obviously, I AM. The basic teaching of any teacher is to meditate on yourself, the witness, and focus your attention on the changeless space that's always there.

There is *no* answer to the question, "From where does this thought arise." However, notice what happens as you ask that question and look for the space from which each thought arises. From where does that thought arise? From where is the thought? If a thought comes by that says "I don't understand," you identify with it and then begin a chain of associations like "I don't understand," "I never understood anything," "this is my story," "oh, my God, what am I going to do, not even meditation works for me." when you identify with anything, you automatically start running the story of your life. The thing to remember is who is the knower and the observer of your thoughts.

I once worked with a married couple in a workshop. The couple had paired up with one another asking each other, "From where does that thought arise?" The woman stopped her enquiring, looked at me, and said, "I'm trying to think of something to say-I'm always trying to think of something to say." I replied, "That's the story of your life," and she answered, "Yes." That thought "I should say something" went by and she identified it as herself. She would then run all her trips about how and why she never knew what she should say. A helpful process for such a person is to ask, "From where does that thought arise?" No matter what thought comes into your awareness, ask, "From where does that thought arise?" Do you feel afraid to get started? Ask yourself, "From where does that thought arise?" As other thoughts arise, keep asking, "From where does that thought arise?"

If there is a thought called "I'm afraid" because when you first came to the thought "I'm afraid," you identified with it and felt like "That's me." Then suddenly your mind said, "I'm afraid because I don't have enough money," "I'm fearful because my relationship is screwed up," "I'm afraid because _(fill in blank)._" The minute you identify with any thought, you have all of the associated psycho-emotional reactions, such as "I'm afraid." And your mind will give you a thousand reasons why you're afraid, or why you should be afraid three weeks from now. Such as, "What if I lose my job," or, "what if the person I'm living with leaves me?" The basic principle of Jnana Yoga is that _you are not your mind._

Nisargadatta Maharaj asked Jean Dunn, who was taping his most recent talk and planning to write a book, "what is the name of my next book?" (As if he could care!) She replied, "Beyond **Consciousness**." He said, "No, no. The name should be _Prior to **Consciousness**,_ prior to your last thought, prior to the thought that you're having, stay there."

Practice: To begin experimenting with this meditation, very gently let your eyes close. The first thing I'd like you to notice is how you are sitting. Notice your hands, where they are physically. I'd like you to notice the rising and falling of your breath. Then, I'd like you to watch the thoughts coming into your awareness. Each time a thought comes through, begin to ask, "From where does this thought arise? From where does this thought arise?"

A student once asked me, "What do I do with experiences that begin to happen?" I answered, "See, you already believe that it's *your* experience. Who told you that?"

I was once sitting with Nisargadatta Maharaj when a psychiatrist and his wife were visiting from France. The psychiatrist asked a very long-winded question about birth and death, going on and on. Maharaj looked at him, then asked, "who told you that you exist?" The psychiatrist looked at his wife and his wife looked at him-I was sitting behind them, and Nisargadatta said, "Your mind tells you 'you' exist. **Consciousness** tells you 'you' exist, and you believe it. If you understand just that, it's enough."

Another person came to Maharaj and said something about birth and death and past and future lives. Maharaj said, "who told you 'you' were born? I didn't know you were born." The visitor replied, "Well, of course I was born. Everyone is born and everyone dies." Maharaj said, "How do you know you're going to die?" He said, "Well, because I was told." Maharaj said. "You don't know you were born, you don't know you're going to die, you believe it to be true, and now you're worried about past lives and future lives and credits and debits. I was never born, and I will never die."

Once a student said to me, "A lot of my experience is not verbal, but I know they are thoughts. Should I bother to put it into words? I feel as if I'm translating into words, and maybe it's not necessary." I commented, "In other words, how do we know we hear anything?" The "I" hears it. It's a thought called "I hear." Everything you experience is translated. Somewhere in your mind is the concept "I hear this." I hear people say, "But that's my experience." Of course it's your experience! You have a thought called, "I don't like this," and identify with it. You say, "Yeah, I don't like that, I can feel it in my solar plexus." Of course you can! You identified with a thought called, "I don't like this," and believed it, and so you can feel it. People believe feelings are more significant; we must understand that feelings, like thoughts, come and go also. For example, one day you meet someone, "fall in love," and sooner or later, you will "fall in hate." Today you wake up and you like the fact that you woke up, and tomorrow you don't. Your feelings like your thoughts are always changing.

In relationships a thought comes by called, "I'm angry with you," and suddenly, I believe it. The next thing I know, I've identified with the thought called "I'm angry with you." My mind will then come up with reasons why. For example, I'm angry with you because you're too tall, or you're too short, or I need less affection, or I need more affection. Remember, you are not the "I." So if I'm in a relationship with you, and I identify with the thought called "I want you to be taller," you might say, "Okay, I'll wear high heels and do my hair up in a bun! " If you buy into my thoughts of you, then they may become your thoughts and then you might imagine that you have to do something about it (my thoughts).

TO WHOM DOES THIS THOUGHT ARISE?

Meditate: *When a thought arises in meditation, ask yourself, "To whom does this thought arise?"*

Answer: *"To me." Then ask, "Who is this 'I'?"*
                                        (Ramana Maharshi)

The purpose of this method is to separate the transient "I's" from the Witnessing Presence, which is always there. The process is as follows: Each time a thought arises ask yourself, "To whom does this thought arise?" Answer to "yourself," "To me." Then ask, "who is this I?" This approach moves the "I" thought from being the subject, to making the "I" thought an object to be witnessed. The "thought" will disappear and another "thought" will appear and take its place.

This process can be done with a partner. Pair up with a partner. Make direct eye contact with them. Whenever a thought comes into the mind, the first person says it out loud. For example, "I don't like it," "I do like it," "it's hot," "it's cold," "I wish I weren't here," whatever the thought is. The second person, sitting opposite, asks the question, "To whom does this thought arise?" The first person responds, "To me," and the second then asks, "who is this I?"

A student asked, "Is there an answer to the question, 'who is this I'?" I replied, "To whom does that thought arise called 'Is there an answer to the question, Who is this I'?" "To me," she replied. I then asked, "who is this I?" She said, "The thought disappeared." Remember, the purpose of the meditation is to move "you" from being the "I" subject, to witnessing the "I" thought as an object. When a thought comes into your mind, ask, "To whom does that thought arise?" Answer, "To me." Ask, "Who is this 'I'?" The process eventually becomes spontaneous and automatic. A student once said, "I don't think I know what I'm doing." I asked him "To whom does that thought arise?" He answered, "To me." I asked, "who is this "I" and said, "Notice that there is a space that opens up after the question 'who is this I?'"

Let's take another example: Imagine a thought that goes by called, "I don't like my friend's looks," and you identify with it, then you'll get to *experience* him that way. If a thought comes by that says, "I don't think I know what I'm doing," and you identify with it, then your mind will start running another trip called, "I never understand what's going on," "why did I come here," "I knew I should have stayed home." Notice how easily thoughts snowball.

To repeat, anything that you believe about yourself is limiting: "I feel good," "I feel bad," "I'm tall, short, fat, thin, ugly." whatever thought comes into mind that you identify with will limit you; it doesn't matter what the content is. "I like it here," "I love myself," "I hate myself"—they are all thoughts. When a thought arises like, "I feel good," ask, "To whom does this thought arise?" Answer, "To me." Then ask, "who is this I?" Begin to notice that there's a space at the end of that question. *Notice that space.*

Practice: Every time a thought comes into your awareness, ask, "To whom does this thought arise?" Answer "To me." Then ask, "who is this I." Witness the experience. Any answer that comes to you, such as, "I am worthless," repeat the process. "To whom does this thought arise?" Answer, "To me." Ask, "who is this I?" Notice the rising and falling of your breathing. Allow yourself to become very relaxed. As any thoughts enter your awareness, continue to ask, "To whom does this thought arise?" Answer, "To me." Then ask, "who is this I?"

When I was in India, I used to start meditation at 3:00 a.m. One morning I was meditating in the cave and a thought came by, "It's an uphill battle all the way." It arose very gently. I looked at it and I asked, "who is this I?" and it disappeared. The truth was that I had experienced my whole life as an uphill battle all the way, which is what my mother had always told me. This assumption about life had been outside of my awareness, and I had never questioned it. Once I questioned this thought it disappeared. I could say that the one major thing Nisargadatta Maharaj had taught me was *how to enquire.*

Meher Baba once described the ego, or the "I" as being like an iceberg. All you can see is 10% of the iceberg and the other 90% of it is under water (unconscious); you can't see it. As you begin to meditate, what is underneath the water starts to come up. You don't have to do anything with it; just notice that it's there. It has nothing to do with who you are. You are the space that witnesses these "I" thoughts.

I remember a student saying, "My concept is, if somebody asks me a question, I answer it." I asked her, "To whom does that thought arise?" She answered, "I don't know, I believed I'm supposed to answer a question, not sit there dumbfounded because I am not able to answer. I am not supposed to go into a space, because I'm not able to answer." I suggested that for the next meditation she *not* go into that space. I asked her to sit there for a few minutes, and not go into the space, I wanted her not to go into that space to see what happened. Of course, by my suggesting she *resist* the space, she fell deeply into meditation.

I remember talking to a student of mine who was saying, "I'm tired," "I don't like my relationship," "I think I should get divorced." I replied, "I... I... I...."

I suggested to him that if a thought goes through

your awareness called, "It's difficult," and you identify with it, your mind will work out a whole story to validate the "I" thought you identified with. "I was never able to do it," "I never could do it," "I knew I shouldn't have come here," "I knew I should have gone to the movies," and on and on. The content of your story doesn't matter. The minute you identify with "It's difficult," that's what your experience has got to be. Suppose you had an opposite reaction-that this is great, and you identify and fuse with that. Then you have an experience of its being great.

Remember, anything you believe will limit you, one way or another. I'm not interested in the content of your **consciousness**; I'm interested in the witness so that the space becomes more available. A thought arises, it subsides, and there's a space. It arises, and it subsides, and there's a space. If a thought comes by that says, "I feel good," and you say, "To whom does this thought arise?" The answer is obvious: "It arises to me." "Who is this I?" The "I feel good" moves from subject thought "I feel good" to object thought "I feel good," and you're immediately witnessing. Anything you witness will disappear. This method stabilizes the witness so that the space between two thoughts gets longer.

A student in one of my classes once said, "My experience is question, blank space, and then there's a search for sound or a search for the key to this thought." My hunch would be that this student's experience, in general, is that he is always searching. Already, he is looking at a pattern and identifying himself as the person who has a pattern. *You are not your patterns.*

Earlier I mentioned the student who said, "I'm trying to think of what to say," that her whole life she's been trying to think of what to say in particular situations. That's one of the patterns that she identifies herself with. She's sitting in a room and a thought comes by called, "what should I say, God, I don't know what to say," and before you know it, she has an anxiety attack. I'm exaggerating this to get the point across. *You are not your patterns.* That's not who you are.

A student said, "It's really weird, because if that isn't who I am, who is there? That's a real weird feeling." I suggested that she was identifying with the patterns of the mind, which are not who she is. Focus on your awareness. Turn your attention away from the content of your mind and notice your awareness because our awareness is always present. This "space" is our beingness, our essence. Unfortunately, instead of being in this "space," what happens is that each of us identifies with the patterns of our mind. Do you feel distracted when you try this exercise? "I'm distracted." That's the pattern you believe you have and are. You decide that these "I" thoughts are pattern repetition. Actually, as a Zen master once said, "You never step in the same river twice." In the same way, each moment is new; we just *believe* that we have a pattern rather than experiencing each moment as new each moment. Furthermore, it is identifying and becoming fascinated with our patterns which enables us to keep from being in the space; *Why?, because the space is our most resisted experience.*

As the thought comes by called "I'm distracted," and you identify with it, the next thing you know your experience is, "I'm distracted, I'm always distracted, I never can focus my attention, I've never been able to meditate, I'm not meditating anymore, this isn't for me." Instead, when the thought comes by called "I'm distracted," you can ask, "To whom does that thought arise?" Answer, "It arises to me." Ask yourself, "who is this I?"

The same thing happened with me, as I mentioned earlier, when a thought came by called, "It's an uphill battle all the way," I identified with it. I grabbed onto it and said to myself, "Yes, my experience of life is an uphill battle." when I saw what I was doing, and let the thought subside and disappear, life was no longer an uphill battle for me. I had never questioned that belief because my experience was that "life was an uphill battle all the way." That was my experience. The thoughts that you identify with will reinforce your experience.

Nisargadatta Maharaj was once talking about birth and death. while he was talking, I remembered images I had in therapy and meditation of being born and dying. when I told him of "my" experience, he looked at me and said, "How did you identify the person in the memory as you?" In other words, the witness had again identified with the memory, and "I" decided I was the person in the movie in my mind.

So I'd like you to sit for about seven to ten minutes, and every time a thought comes into your awareness, ask yourself, "To whom does this thought arise?" The answer: "To me." And then ask yourself, "who is this I?" And notice what happens.

Practice: Again, you don't have to think of an answer. I'd like you to let your eyes close very gently. Notice the way you're sitting. As thoughts arise in "your" **consciousness**, I'd like you to begin to ask, "To whom does this thought arise?" Answer, "To me." Then ask, "Who is this I?" and notice what happens.

A student commented, "There was so much space that the words didn't make a lot of sense. Before I could ask about the thought, it was gone, so I couldn't remember it. It's weird, there's such value placed on thoughts, and then they can't be remembered two seconds later." Another student commented, "I guess I realized how we put too much into concepts. It was like trying to break away from an umbilical cord." I replied, "You're shifting your awareness from identification with 'I subject' to 'I object'." Asking the question, "Who is this I?" automatically shifts your awareness from your identification with "I subject," to witnessing the "I" thought as an object.

Meditate: *Focus your attention and witness all of the "pseudo I's"*
(Vijnana Bhairava, Jaideva Singh)

I'd like you to sit for seven to ten minutes. What you're probably experiencing is the "pseudo-I's," which is all the "I's" such as "I like this" and "I don't like this," "I feel good," "I feel bad," or "I feel happy or sad," whatever those "I's" are, we're going to refer to them in this meditation as "pseudo-I's." They're coming and going and always changing.

We're going to focus our attention on the space, on the permanent "I" that watches all the "pseudo-I's," which is what we have been doing, except that now we are going to remove the technique of enquiry for about seven to ten minutes. Simply focus your attention on the "I" that witnesses all of the "pseudo-I's." If you get stuck and are not able to do that, then move into the self-enquiry, "To whom does this thought arise?" Answer, "To me." Then ask, "Who is this I?" Both enquiries lead to the same point of focusing and *witnessing* and not identifying with the "pseudo-I's."

Meditate: *Focus on the thought-free "I," the Presence behind all of the "pseudo-I's."*
(Vijnana Bhairava, Jaideva Singh)

Practice: About seven to ten minutes.
Notice the sounds around you. Feel your body pressed against the seat. Begin to focus on the thought-free "I", the pres-

ence behind all of the "pseudo-I's." Notice whatever sounds are around you; again focus your attention on the thought-free "I," the presence behind all the "pseudoI's." Continue to focus your attention on the thought-free "I", the presence behind all the "pseudo-I's". Very gently, bring your awareness back to the room, and whenever you're ready, let your eyes open.

ALL INFORMATION COMES FROM THE MIND

Meditate: *When a thought arises ask, 'Who told you that?" then answer: "The mind."*

The purpose of this practice is to cultivate the understanding that all information comes from the mind. To emphasize this, since it is the nature of the mind to always change its mind, it is apparent that one must understand that thoughts are the mind. By practicing this meditation, the identification with the "mind stuff" loosens its grip. Nisargadatta Maharaj used to say, "To go beyond the mind you must look away from the mind and its contents."

This practice is first done with a partner. Each time a thought arises, ask yourself, "Who told you that?" Then answer, "The mind." Whenever anything comes into your awareness, the question will be asked of you by a partner, "Who told you that?" and the answer is, "The mind." The only way you could possibly know that you are feeling or experiencing is if the voice in the back of your head says, "I'm happy," or "I'm sad," or whatever. Whatever you know about, you get told through your mind.

A student asked, "why is it *the* mind?" I replied, "Because the mind is made of thoughts. Thoughts that you identify with, you make *my* thoughts. So, really, it's *the* mind and *the* thoughts. when you identify with thoughts, you make them *my* mind or *my* thoughts." Also, for the seeding for future understanding, there is only *one* mind, not *many* minds. Working with *the* mind begins to cultivate the next level of awareness, i.e., *there is only one mind.*

Practice: I'd like you to sit for about seven to ten minutes and notice each thought as it comes through your awareness. The mind might say, "It's hot, it's cold, I don't understand." I want to make it clear that if a thought comes by that says, "I don't understand" and you identify and fuse with it, then you immediately have an experience called, "I don't understand, I never understood, I wish I understood, why is it always me?"

The aim is to not identify with anything that comes through your mind. Remember that it's the nature of the mind to always change its mind. If you're in a relationship, one day you're happy with it, and the next day you re not. One day you like where you live, the next day you don't.

There's a book written by a woman saint, Ananda Mayi Ma, who died about August 1982. when people asked her a question, she always said, "The body thinks, or the mind thinks," rather than, "I think."

ANY THOUGHTS CAN BE OBJECTIFIED

Meditate: *When a thought arises, objectify it and witness it.*

(*Vijnana Bhairava,* Jaideva Singh)

In the next meditation anything that comes into your awareness, separate from it and witness it from a distance, like it is an object. This means to simply witness it as you would a chair, a picture, or a table. "I feel good," for example, can be separated from and observed from a distance like you might look at a table. "I like being here" can be separated from and witnessed from a distance like you might see a chair. "I wish I weren't here" can be separated from and witnessed from a distance like you might look at a picture. "I feel a lot of love" can be separated from and witnessed from a distance like you might look at a pair of shoes. I remember in a meditation group I taught, a student said that he was feeling a lot of bliss with this exercise. He said that he separated from and witnessed from a distance the bliss and it shifted his awareness to a space where he had never been before. Usually, we take a feeling like bliss and identify with it and say, "I'm in bliss," but he was able to separate from and observe it from a distance as an object. So the purpose of the next exercise is to separate from and observe from a distance anything that comes into your awareness and just witness it, no matter what it is.

A student asked me, "If I'm watching my breath, would I say, 'She is watching her breath,' using third-person?" I replied that, yes, you could make it third person. Instead of saying, for example, "I am watching my breath," you could say, "She is watching her breath." You can objectify and witness from a distance the breathing process.

Notice what the experience is. And if the mind says, "This is a far out experience," then you want to separate from "This is a far out experience" and witness it from a distance. "This is a neat experience." The next thought is "I really like doing this, that feels neat" and you start feeling "neat." Shift "I feel neat" and separate from it and observe it from a distance as an object.

Practice: Begin by sitting and watching your breathing. Whatever experience or thought comes through your awareness, separate from it and witness it from a distance as an object so that you're witnessing that thought or experience that comes through your awareness. Now very gently, separate from and witness from a distance anything that comes up for you. Whatever thoughts or feelings or experiences that you're having, move them and make them an object to be witnessed. Whatever thoughts or experiences you have, separate from them and witness them from a distance as an object.

A student once said to me after this meditation, "I was immediately drawn into a beingness or an energy and then that energy expanded. I was able to disappear into that energy so that all that was there was the energy. I was not there."

When I was working with Nisargadatta Maharaj, I felt like I was going crazy because I had all this stuff going on with me, and I kept trying to witness it, or do something like that. I said to him, "Am I thinking more, or am I witnessing more?" He answered, "You're witnessing more, it is just a phase." I said, "It's a long phase." *He didn't laugh.* Working this way with yourself allows more space for other things to come into awareness, which makes it appear as thought there are more thoughts to come into "your" mind which normally are controlling you from outside your awareness.

TO WHERE DOES THAT THOUGHT SUBSIDE?

Meditate: *Each time a thought arises ask, "To where does that thought subside?"*

A student began a group with the comment, "I notice that my perspective has changed. Things don't seem to have the same weight." This meditation is to notice where that thought subsides to. It arises and subsides into space. This question will bring you to that *same* space.

This teaching is from Ramana Maharshi, the twentieth-century sage and teacher of self-enquiry. A thought arises and subsides: Notice to where that thought subsides. Is there an answer to that question? No. We're noticing the space. Once you're in that space, there won t be anything. There will be nothing. Then another thought will arise called, "I don't know if I got it or not." Notice where that thought subsides to.

A student asked for a comment on images coming in because he found them to be the only thing that was coming that he was aware of. He thought perhaps he should be analyzing the images and thought them to be a continuous stream of input, without pauses. I told this student to slow the process down so that it was like frames of a movie. In the same way, if you slow down a film strip, what you have is the space between frames, which you could jump through. That's the understanding. It appears like a stream of very connected **consciousness**, but actually there is a space from which it arises, and to which it subsides back.

A man came to Nisargadatta and described the Insight (Vipassana) meditation he was doing, and Nisargadatta started yelling at him. The translator said, "You have to understand that whatever you say you re doing or experiencing, Maharaj will say, *'That's not it.'* No matter what it is, that's not it. You always have to keep noticing, 'Where does that thought subside to,' because there's a space from which it all arises and to which it subsides, and that's the space you're looking for. There are no qualities to it. Anything you imagine it is, *is not it.* So, notice where does that thought subside to."

Practice: Sit for seven to ten minutes with your eyes closed.

As thoughts come into your awareness, begin to notice, "where does that thought subside to." Follow the thought to the space where it subsides. There will be a space and then another thought will arise. Watch it. To where does that thought subside? when you're ready, come back slowly and open your eyes.

A student commented, "It seemed as if I was in that space primarily, and then there were thoughts going on, but I couldn't pay attention to them. It wasn't as if I was in the space between the thoughts but that the thoughts were somewhere out there. Rather than focusing on them, and identifying with them, it was as if I was drawn to get away from them."

Another student explained, "I found that I'd have a thought and I noticed 'To where does that thought subside.' I then felt as if I couldn't watch to see where it had gone. Then I remembered that you had said to stay in the space and that the question was a method. Then I was at peace." This student was right: The question is supposed to *bring you back*. Many times, you'll find you've been tripping out and all of a sudden you've been to Hawaii, been on vacation, had a love affair, and you'll come back and realize that a minute of meditation has gone by. To where does that thought subside?

WHOSE THOUGHTS ARE THESE?

Meditate: *Each time a thought arises, ask, "Whose thoughts are these?"*

Practice: I want you to meditate for seven to ten minutes. All I want you to do is watch the thoughts that stream through your awareness. Ask yourself, "Whose thoughts are these?" Thoughts are always going by from the one mind. For some of them you're saying, "That's me," and for others you're saying, "That's not me." I want you to ask "Whose thoughts are these?" They're streaming through. Again, it's a matter of noticing what's coming in. See what happens as you ask yourself that for a few minutes. Continue to ask yourself, "Whose thoughts are these? Whose thoughts are these?" Begin to witness them. Just witness.

A student reacted, "At first it was fun because I had a mixture of thoughts on a line that I could think about. Then I started worrying about the effect of my thoughts and if I were responsible for them, and it all fell apart." I asked her, "Whose thoughts are these? You can't *control* the thoughts you're going to have five or ten minutes from now, so why try to control them now?" Swami Prakashananda once said, "You can't even control very much the next time you're going to go to the bathroom. So, let happen what happens. You watch."

Another student said, "I started having the weird sensation-I wasn't thinking very verbally-that the self was a thought, the body was a thought, and the sound was a thought. At first I thought, no, this is awareness; but then I thought you can use any word you like but there's no difference between a verbal thought that my head comes up with and this sofa that I'm sitting on." I said, "You're right: the sofa is a little more solid, but it is still a thought."

Another student commented, "You know we've been working on things like sadness and fear and how you can let emotions evaporate by concentrating on them. How do you deal with guilt?" I said, first you have to know what guilt is. *Guilt is resentment turned against yourself.* So first you have to straighten out the energy. In other words, if I resent somebody or something, and I don't express that resentment, it's retroflected back on me. That means that rather than expressing my resentment, I put it back on myself and what I get is *guilt.*

If I were to feel guilty; the first thing I would do to

straighten out the energy is to start off sentences with, "I resent _____," then fill in the blank. That will at least turn the energy around so that you'll start turning it toward the person or object which you are resenting. That's one way to do it. It can be that simple. If it's depression, it's more than likely anger turned against yourself or a *resisted experience.* So, either feel the anger or notice what experience you are resisting-then experience the resisted experience. Resentment is a little bit lighter than depression. The deeper the depression, the more you have been putting anger back on yourself or the more you have a *resisted experience.* In Sanskrit, depression is defined as lack of *shakti* or lack of *"energy."* "E" means outward, *emotion* is outward motion. When you have the emotion and don't express it or feel it, *it takes a lot of energy to resist an emotion,* hence, depression.

WHO IS WITNESSING?

Meditate: *When a thought arises ask, "Who is witnessing?" The answer: "I am."*

If you look at your experiences, you'll see that you are always witnessing your thoughts: who is the witness of your thoughts? I am. Who is the witness of your experience? I am. who is the witness of everything that happens? I am. Eventually, what you'll start seeing is that the I AM is also a concept. It's kind of a quantum leap; it's another belief. *You believe that you exist sepa-*

rate from other people or things. That's where all your
problems come from!

In Nisargadatta's book called *Seeds of Consciousness,* he says, "Once you believe I AM, then you
believe, 'I am a man,' 'I am a woman' and 'I have all
this other stuff that I have to do,' and believe 'I need
this' and 'I need that.' So we can try to nip it right at I
AM."

Maharaj's premise is that you start from I AM and
use the I AM as a *pointer,* understanding it is the *seed of
your personal consciousness.*

A student asked me, "what if the I AM doesn't feel
as if it means anything?" I replied, "It doesn't. It's a
concept." The student answered, "But it's really disori-
enting to be alive in the physical plane, always feeling
that you don't exist." I replied, "You believe that you
exist separate from everything else. who is separate?
You still believe that you are separate. That's where the
conflict is." "Well, it would be hard to function if you
didn't believe that you were separate," he said. I said,
"In other words, you are saying, 'It's hard for *me* to
function; I can't do it.' There's still an 'I' that you're
identifying with."

You can identify with a concept like, "It's hard for
me to function. Oh, my God, it's so hard; I'm disoriented," and all of the other stuff. Anything you believe
will limit you. That's why I do my best not to give any
concepts-because if you identify with "It's difficult, I
feel disoriented," then what you get to experience is dis-
orientation because the thought comes first. There is a

Sufi practice where you live your life trying to experience no separation from anything else.

Once you identify with anything, it's going to limit you: "I feel good, I feel bad. I like it here, I don't like it here." You can identify with your own separate existence. Or you can witness, "I exist, or I don't exist." In the *Avadhut Stotram* it is said that someone in that *no-state state* has no need to accept or reject and is in an experience that is beyond attributes, qualities, and is beyond the concept existence and nonexistence. In Hindu philosophy there are four states: waking, dream, deep sleep, and then the transcendent which is called "Turiya," the witness of the other three. I had many experiences years ago in which I thought I was not sleeping, but then looked at my clock when "I" awoke and saw that hours had gone by. Suddenly I realized that I was the witness of my deep sleep state. I realized then that I don't sleep; the body and mind sleep. That's the fourth state. To someone in that state of awareness, everything (waking, dreaming, and deep sleep) is all the same, because such a person is in a constant, uninterrupted state of pure awareness.

Upon hearing this, a student asked me whether things happened to the "I" during the sleep state. I replied, during deep sleep, the "I" doesn't even exist. To a *Vedantan,* whether it be dream, sleep, or waking state, it rises and subsides and then there is a space. To a Jnani, the only thing that's real is that which is *permanent;* what is unreal is that which is *transient.* Consequently, what is *permanent and real* is beyond the witness and what is *transient and unreal* is everything else.

A student asked me if we could use another word for "witness," perhaps "soul." I said, "I really don't want to get too theoretical; I would rather you meditate and have an "experience." Then you can work it out for yourself. To me, a soul would only mean where your impressions are all held. That's all. It's still in time and space, and it still has a beginning, a middle, and an end. The question to ask yourself is, who is the knower and witness of the soul? I've seen what is called my causal body or soul. Who is the witness of the causal body? Who is watching the causal body? Who is always there? Because the causal body has to have a beginning, a middle, and an end.

I was hanging out with Swami Prakashananda Maharaj in about 1978. A woman came to him because she had been seeing certain different colored lights in meditation. She wanted to know what it meant. He spoke for a long time about all these different-colored lights and then said, "It doesn't matter what lights you see. The question is, who is *witnessing* these lights? *Find out.*"

The causal body is the deep sleep body; it holds all of your impressions. A student asked me if it was the deep self. "Well," I said, "it's a level: it's a deeper level of individual self, but it is still the *individual self.* The causal body holds all of the impressions. Who is the witness of that?" I have had a lot of experiences watching my causal body; I was watching myself die, and then I watched myself be reborn. I watched my causal body do all kinds of things, and then I came to understand by enquiring, "what witness is witnessing that," that I was beyond the witness of my causal body and that I am what is real and permanent and that my causal body arises and subsides in the **EMPTINESS**.

"I" was witnessing it. "I" was always there witnessing. "I" was the witness. Otherwise, you're the one that you think was born and died and was reborn. But who's the witness of birth and death if you look into your experience? What I would always ask myself is, "Can I recall a time when I didn't exist?" If you really look into your experience, it's not very mystical: You always were. You can either meditate on yourself, which always is, or you can meditate on everything that's changing and goes up and down, and up and down.

I've been asked. "What is the function of the self in the universe?" "In ten words or less? I have no answer for that." The mind wants meaning. That's the nature of the mind. But who is witnessing that? Sometimes, a lot of frustration and upset comes in all that. It can be very painful. who is witnessing that? Someone once asked Nisargadatta Maharaj, "Is there a purpose to life?" He replied, *"No,* next question."

Practice: The question I want you to ask yourself, for seven to ten minutes whenever anything arises in your mind is, "who is witnessing?" Then answer "I AM." Every time a thought comes through, "Who is witnessing?" "I AM." "Who is witnessing?" "I AM." For about ten minutes. You can verbalize it if you need to.

"My" students have found that these meditation techniques have opened many questions they thought they had buried. One student told me, "I feel like it's a process of finding myself going back into old patterns that I thought were long gone; they keep popping up, one after another."

As a thought comes through, ask, "who is witnessing?" Answer, "I AM."

REGARDING PAST LIVES

A guy came to see me for regular therapy, and all of these things ended up in past lives. He started telling me about them, and I said, "what's really important, if I am going to work on it at that level, is I would want to know what I brought from past lives into this life, not the story-I was King Arthur, and therefore I like to duel." what's important is the pattern of behavior which I repeat now, *not the story*.

I was once with Nisargadatta Maharaj and I began remembering "past lives." He asked me what I saw. I said that it was a memory, which looked like a cinema, i.e., I was doing this or that and other people were doing this or that. He asked me to consider two questions:

1. Who is the knower of the knowledge of your birth? Find out.

2. How did you decide of all the people in the memory the one that was you?
Find out.

My friend went to see a past-life therapist for a session. The therapist got him back to some past life and my friend was saying, "Yeah, it's like I can see myself; I'm going across the wilderness, and it's about 1850. I see the covered wagon." The therapist was saying, "That's good, keep describing what you're seeing." My friend continued, "And my wife and I were going across...," he was describing all of the hardships he went through. The past-life therapist says, "As you're going farther and farther west, keep describing it." And they're going on and on. Finally, the therapist says, "who are you, what's your name?" And he says, "Levi-Strauss." I swear to God. Gimme a break. The past-life therapist says, "I really believe he was Levi-Strauss." Sure you were.

I've seen some of my own "past lives." Another time, Nisargadatta Maharaj asked me, "How did you experience past lives in your mind?" I said, "I saw a film, a movie in my mind, of people gathered around, and I had died and was reborn." He asked me, "How did you know the person that died was you? Find out how did you decide to identify to the person in the movie and then decide it was *you*. How was it that the witness picked this one to identify with? Find that out." That's a much greater issue.

"WHO IS THIS I?"

When you are beginning this meditation, it is sometimes helpful to work with another person. *One* person says her or his thoughts, however odd they seem, and the *other person* asks the question: "who is this I?" and then the other person notices their experience.

Once in a class, as I was beginning this exercise, a student said, "It made me really angry, this whole thing, not the work we are doing, but what it essentially brings up. I am really angry that I don't know who I am." I told this student, "Before you find out who you are, I think first you have to understand that you don't know who you are." He continued: "Is there ever a point in existence where you know who you are?" "I" answered that "I" knew who "I" was, and that "I" wouldn't be doing this work if "I" didn't. He replied, "It was a relief because that's my hope, that I can find that out; otherwise, I'd say forget it. I'd rather go into oblivion because I'm getting sick of the whole thing." Ignorance isn't bliss, ignorance is dullness. You will find out who you are, eventually. But start by asking yourself, "who is this I?"

There's a saying in the *Upanishads:* "The dawn of knowledge is when you realize that you're ignorant." when you realize you don't know who you are, that is the dawn of knowledge. Before then, you assume that the world is the way you imagine it to be. Everybody has different perspectives, a little bit of programming here and there. Asking, "who is this I?" is peeling the onion. Who is this I? I'm not this, I'm not this. I'm certainly not the things my parents told me I was. Who am I then?

A student once complained to me, "You can't have an experiential sense of who you are." You're having it all the time but you don't experience it because you are identifying with your individual minds. Who you are actually is experienced as a non-experience experience. Before we actually sit down and do this practice, remember that the thought you have, if you think about it or look at it, is separate from you. Therefore, *you are not your thoughts*. Who are you then? Find out.

A student asked, "Supposing you reach a place that you sense who you are, do you make it not you again?" I answered, "Yes. There's no *quality* to it. It's not good or bad or high or low or right or wrong, or fat or thin, or man or woman. The sense of is-ness, which is always there-that's who you are, unless you want to identify with something else. It is beyond attributes and beyond qualities, and it's right here all the time. That is why it goes unnoticed."

It doesn't feel good or bad. Did I enjoy this workshop? The truth of the matter is I don't know if I enjoyed the workshop, only Identities or the "I" knows that. I'm not happy, I'm not unhappy. Stephen goes up and down, but I'm not Stephen; if I want to identify with being Stephen, then I can go up and down. People want to be in a happy state and be a happy person in that *state*. This man came to Nisargadatta Maharaj and said, "I want to be happy." Maharaj replied, "That's nonsense, happiness is where the 'I' isn't." What happens loses significance. It's like after you've eaten food, you don't think about where it goes. In the same way life becomes like that. You don't think about it. There is no longer any *inner considering,* you just *are* and *do.*

When students asked Maharaj why he smoked cigarettes (he used to smoke cigarettes and drink a lot of tea), he said, "Years ago, I left my human nature to look after itself. what does that have to do with me? why should I care?" Remember, anything you identify with will limit you.

A student commented, "I guess what goes on with me is that I'm so sick of playing this game, and I'm hoping that, at some point, not that it has to prove this or that, but that it feels okay, to be aware that it's worth it, you know, the whole bother about things." I told her that, again, she believed that she was Janey or Sue instead of Laura or Michelle. She believed that she was having all of this material going on with her.

You can get into a great state of meditation, but unless the psychological and emotional issues are really clear, you will immediately identify with your issues. Everybody does until they understand that's not who they are. It's interesting: *we've been hypnotized, all of us. and actually the whole game is about becoming dehypnotized.* I like that way of putting it. So we're going to dehypnotize ourselves. We're going to go beyond the normal hypnosis of "I'm Becky" or "I'm Bill."

If you start asking, "who is this I?" and you continue in that line, the process forces the "I" to move from subject "I" to object "I." Once the "I" is witnessed, it disappears, and there's nothing but space. That "I" doesn't exist anymore. It's like when you go to bed at night. Does the "I" exist? "Wait a second," a student asked, *"how does this work?"* Ask yourself, "who is this 'I' that wants to *know?"* Remember *anything you know can not be you.*

The basic principle of Kashmir Shaivism, which is the second aphorism of the *Shiva Sutras,* is *Jnanam bandhah:* "Knowledge is bondage." It says that anything you know (about yourself or the world) will bind you. You think you're smart; you think you're dumb; you think you're weak; you think you're strong; you think you're unlovable; you think you're spiritual; you think you're worthless. Whatever it is, what you know about yourself will limit. Knowledge therefore is bondage.

WHO TOLD YOU THAT?

Meditate: *When a thought arises ask yourself "Who told you that?" Then answer: "The mind."*

The question for this meditation is, "who told you that?" The answer is, "The mind," not MY mind, but THE mind. Everything you know about yourself comes through the mind, because you wouldn't know if you were happy or sad or if you felt good or bad or if you liked someone or if you didn't unless it was from something in your mind telling you it is so. So when a thought comes through your awareness and tells you that you like someone or hate someone or that you feel good or bad, you ask yourself, "Who told you that?" Then you answer, "The mind."

The purpose of this exercise is to become clear that it's the mind. The mind tells you that you feel good, and *you believe it;* the mind tells you that you feel bad, and *you believe it.* There's nothing personal about it. It is *the mind.* It is the nature of the mind to always change its mind. It is its nature. It's like your nature to be what *you* are; it's the mind's nature to be what *it* is. It is not personal. The difference between *the* mind and *my* mind is a very subtle one. If you were to say my mind," the assumption is that you are solid, and it belongs to you. Rather *the mind* and *there are thoughts;* in this way it becomes easier not to fuse with thoughts but to witness them.

East Indian literature says that the key to freedom lies in renunciation. what do we mean by renunciation? Do you have to give up our desires or your feelings? No. You have to give up your identification with them or with the identification with "I," "me," "mine." That's true renunciation. So you have to give up identification with the mind. It means that you no longer identify yourself as the mind or with the functioning of the mind. The most important thing to understand is that the "I" will always run its tape. When I had lived in

India for a long time, people would leave and come back and I would still be there. After six years, someone came up to me and said, "You'll be here forever" (as if I was something special). "Actually, I'm leaving in June" I said. They said, "Oh, that's your ego." I replied, "I used to have an ego called 'I want to stay.' Now 'I' have an ego called 'I want to leave.' They are both *ego.*" It is all ego, *"I* love God" is ego—"I hate God" is ego—"I want to do service" is ego—"I hate doing service" is ego. They believed that one "I" thought was ego, and one "I" thought was not. It is very important to remember this: that all "I" thoughts are still "I" thoughts. Otherwise you get hooked into believing "I feel great" or "I love life" *is not* ego, whereas "I hate life" *is* ego. Anything after "I" is ego and therefore it will change.

Practice: I'd like you to meditate for about seven to ten minutes. Every time a thought comes into your awareness, no matter what it is, ask, "Who told you that?" and then answer, "It is the mind." See what happens. It's the mind: it's not you. Nonverbal thoughts or images, whatever you experience: *"It's the mind."*

A student asked, "How can you have any kind of an experience if you don't have an awareness of it?" Well, who is aware of these things? If the experience is sad, you can ask, "Okay, who told me that?" The mind told me it is sadness. You can change the phraseology of it to say, "who told you that you were aware?" The mind told you that you were aware. When a student commented that this exercise was more difficult than the earlier ones had been, I reminded her that we had only sat for about seven to ten minutes and that while I had been sitting for hours a day for years, the first few minutes were still often the most difficult. I went to Nisargadatta Maharaj and kept asking him questions about this, and he said, "Let your mind do whatever it wants to. You stay out of it and watch."

At the beginning, we sometimes feel we are stabilizing in witnessing but still have a long way to go. We are *planting seeds;* part of this whole workshop is to plant seeds. Witnessing is witnessing is witnessing. In 1990, Dr. Peter Madill sent me some audio tapes he had of Nisargadatta Maharaj. Maharaj was saying on the tapes what I had been experiencing and teaching for *years,* yet I do not remember him ever saying these things in all the time I was there. At some level, however, he was *planting seeds.*

FIND THE "I" IN THE BODY

Meditate: *As you watch your thoughts, look for the "I" in the body.*

Practice: As you watch your thoughts, try to find the "I" in the body. Look for it. See what happens as you look for it. Let us practice for about ten minutes.

A student pointed out after doing this exercise that he had a hard time staying awake. Many people, when they start meditating think they have gone to sleep. I've heard many students say they were falling asleep, because the mind gets very relaxed.

A student asked, "what does it say if I can't find the 'I' in my body?" I said, "Maybe it's not there!" "Is that good or bad?" she said. I responded that I didn't experience it as either. Another student found that there was "a desperation inside the body **consciousness** to identify with something." I responded by saying, "Part of the nature of the mind is to want to identify with something." Another student commented, "I had a sense of peace, and there was a feeling of, 'Okay, we know what this game is about. This game is about showing that the "I" is not in the body. And so we'll go along with that game, but as soon as we walk out the door, we're going to know that the "I" is in the body!'" I told this student that Swami Muktananda once told a story about people that bathe in the Ganges, and their sins are washed away. But the sins go up into the trees, so after you come out of the water, they jump back on you from the trees.

This is the problem with stabilizing in the no-state state. In meditation, I could sit quietly and enter into the void. Shortly after I arose, however, my mind would come back. Actually, "you" (CONSCIOUSNESS at one level, the nervous system at another level), condenses down to form the mind again.[1]

---

[1]This is discussed more fully in *Quantum Consciousness* and in the trilogy entitled, *The Way of the Human.*

THE TRANSMUTATION
OF ENERGY

3 / THE TRANSMUTATION OF ENERGY

Transmutation can be defined as a change in condition or alteration, as in qualities or states of mind. In alchemy, transmutation is the changing of base metals into silver or gold. In biology; it is the changing of one species into another: i.e., *evolution*. In chemistry; it is the *conversion* of one element into another. *Transmutation:* to change from one form into another form.

To the self-explorer, therapist, spiritual aspirant, or the individual exploring self-awareness, it is imperative to understand what freezes and holds emotions, events, or situations so they are experienced the way they are. To illustrate, anger without a label is "energy" or **consciousness** in a form different from sadness. Sadness is energy in a form different from hate. Once experienced without labels and judgments, the steps of transmutation are easily accomplished. First, remove the label from the sensation, emotion etc., and second, witness or watch the experience with no judgment, evaluation or significance placed upon it. Just experience it as "energy" or **consciousness**.

This is an effortless process. *Consciousness transmutes itself* This is not a process of effort or changing one thing into another because an individual "imagines" this or that is better, for here lies the subtle judgment, which freezes, holds and locks the experience in space and time. Normally, psychology leaves us in the predicament of either expressing or repressing feelings that are judged, through prior learning, as bad or unwanted. Transmutation affords the self-explorer or therapist the opportunity to add a third alternative to the expression-repression continuum, namely *transmutation.*

Merely by witnessing or watching emotions, thoughts, feelings, etc., as they are, namely "energy" or **consciousness**, the "experience" transmutes itself.

As I begin this chapter, I want to emphasize the only concept that feels comfortable and applicable to introduce in this book is that everything is made of "energy" or **consciousness** in different shapes or forms, i.e., thoughts, ideas, fantasies, and objects. The purpose of the following meditations is to help you to allow for the transmutation of all your experience so that psychoemotional energies are experienced as the pure "energy" of **consciousness**, thus freeing "you."

FEAR

Meditate: *Focus your attention on the emotion rather than on the story of why you feel the emotion; experience the emotion as made of "energy."*

The basic idea of placing your attention on the emotion comes from the *Vijnana Bhairava,* which is one of the major texts in Kashmir Shaivism. It contains *dharanas,* which are Tantric practices. *Dharana* is defined as fixing your attention on a set point. Tantra means the expansion of knowledge. To sum up this practice, the *Tantra Asana* says, "One rises by that which one falls." I realized that taking the label off of the emotion and experiencing it as "energy" led to a transmutation. Simply stated, a transmutation takes place when you focus your attention on an emotion *"as made of energy or **consciousness**."*

Actually, the first set of exercises will focus on emotions as "energy." The second set on the observer of the emotion and all objects as being made of the same **consciousness**.

For example, when you feel afraid, your mind will give you about twenty reasons why you're afraid. Normally, people focus their attention on the story about why they are afraid. Rather than doing that, I would like you to take your attention off of the story or reason of why you feel fear, and focus your attention on the fear itself: where is the fear in your body? Begin to focus your attention on the fear itself.

This meditation is about learning how to *transmute* energy. Sex is the easy one to talk about; if you have a sexual fantasy, and you focus your attention on the sexual fantasy, you get a bodily reaction of some sort. You keep fantasizing and begin to look outside yourself for this fantasy to be fulfilled. I started reading the *Vijnana Bhairava* 25 years ago. To paraphrase one of the *dharanas* or meditations: From the memory of touching, pressing or kissing, there's a delightful feeling that arises, but since there's nobody there, then, obviously, the feeling comes from *inside you.*

This is very profound. Since there is no one in your room during a fantasy, then the feeling comes from *inside you.* If you take your attention off of the fantasy, away from the story, and focus your attention on the feeling itself, then when you take the label off of the emotion and experience it as energy, it begins to transmute itself, or, to say it another way: *The emotion is already made of energy but how you experience it is transmuted.* Take off the label called fear, and experience it as energy. If a tight chest is an indication to you that you are afraid, then focus your attention on your tight chest as *contracted energy.* In other words, your chest may be tight when you feel afraid. For somebody else, it might be in the pit of their stomach, in their heart, in their hands. So we are going to focus on the emotion rather than the object of emotion or the story about what you're afraid of.

Hopefully, from doing this exercise, we will find out for ourselves that fear or anger or joy or happiness, whatever emotion, *is* energy in a different form. The *Shiva Sutras* would say that it's all **consciousness**, but what's important is that everything is made out of the *same substance;* all is **consciousness**, energy; or *shakti.*

Practice: I'd like you to begin by developing a fantasy of a past event or a future something that you're imagining will happen that is associated with fear. It could have been last week; it could have been last month; it could have been last year. I'd like you to let a memory of something you're afraid of come into your mind. I'd like you to notice what kind of clothes you are wearing, what color they are. Notice if there are any other people in the movie in your mind. Experience any sounds you hear in the movie. I'd like you to notice that feeling of fear that you have. Where is it in your body? I would like you to let your memory really develop. Notice the feeling of that fear that you have. Now at the moment that the fear is at a high point of intensity, I'd like you to take your attention away from the memory and focus it on the fear itself, or the emotion itself. Notice where in your body your feeling of fear is. I'd like you to focus your attention on the fear in your body. Where is it? Where does it sit physically? Every time your mind wants to go back to the memory about *why* you're afraid, focus it gently back onto the feeling of the fear itself. I want you to begin to view that fear as simply energy in a different form. See the fear as energy. See your emotion as energy and allow the energy to do what it does. *Do not try to change it.*

On emerging from this meditation, a student once said that his head felt sensitive, with a sense of energy passing through it. He said, "My head feels real different from the rest of me." I asked if his head felt open at the top, and he replied that it did. "It feels as if there's so much energy in it, it is expanding."

When I was in India in about 1977, I was sitting at 5:30 in the morning one day in May, and chanting Sanskrit mantras. It was probably about 110⁰F. I was feeling incredibly angry. I stopped what I was doing (my mind was thinking up reasons why I was angry—it's hot, it's crowded, and so on). I put my chanting book down and focused my attention on my anger. To paraphrase a tantric text called the *Spanda Karikas,* when you're feeling extremely happy or extremely joyful, or extremely sad or angry, or you are running for your life, if at that moment you could become introverted, you would experience *Spanda,* which is the divine pulsation. Of course, what they leave out is, if at that moment you could *remember* to become introverted! When I focused on the anger as energy, and took the label off and experienced it as energy, I went into bliss. This is what can happen with this exercise. What is critical, however, is that you must experience the emotion as energy *without the intention of getting rid of it.* If you are trying to get rid of it, *you are resisting it,* which keeps it there.

Practice: In the memory in your mind, notice the people and where you are physically. Notice as the feeling of fear begins to arise, or sensations associated with the fear arise. As you watch your memory, notice if there are any sounds, maybe people's voices, and continue to watch the movie called "fear." Allow the feeling to be there, and the physical tension that might be there, notice.

Very gently pull your attention away from the story called "fear." Move it into the fear itself. Find where the fear is in your body. It might have a color or a shape, but witness the energy called "fear," witnessing it as energy in a different form. Continue to witness the energy in your body; notice if it moves. Keep your attention on the emotion of energy: Watch the energy. Gently, notice where your body is physically, and your breath, and bring your attention back to the room whenever you're ready.

I asked a class whether anyone had been able to feel any fear. One student answered, "I went through the whole physical sensation of the tight stomach, and the nausea and the prickles on the face—you know, the loss of control and short breath. I went through all that, but then I tried to say, 'where's that fear coming from,' and then my mind sort of shut."

I reminded him that the mind will come up with many reasons why you're afraid. However, you can take your attention from the justification, the story about why you're afraid, and I know you all feel you have a good reason to feel afraid! It takes some practice to move your attention away from the story to the *fear itself.* It means you have to let go of the story or be willing to let go of the story. But move your attention from the story about why you're afraid into the fear itself. Some students have said that they could only let go of the story enough to watch what the fear was doing in various parts of their bodies, but could not get far enough away from the story to watch the fear as a form of energy. Once again, I reminded the group that we are planting seeds.

The fear loses a lot of power when you turn your attention into it and focus on it, and you can begin to use the power of that energy. *Rather than try to get rid of emotions such as fear, as most kinds of therapy suggest, you can begin to utilize them as energy.*

You will be amazed once you are able to do this a couple of times in your life. When I first did it, I was feeling incredibly angry. When I dropped the story—

and I had no reason in the world to be angry and the mind was popping up reasons—and I really stopped and turned my attention inside, I was in ecstasy in about five seconds. From that point on, I understood, *experientially,* how to begin to work with transmuting the energy of emotions or transmuting my experience of the emotions.

As you begin to turn your attention in and it is a practice because you are turning habitual attention around, it will start happening on its own. It's comparable to learning a sport. At first you might feel very awkward, but after a while, it starts happening in and of itself. You get into a swimming pool, and you don't have to think about swimming, you swim. You don't have to think about holding your breath when you go underwater, you do it. As you practice, it comes quite spontaneously.

Step 1: Recall a time you felt afraid.

Step 2: Notice where in your body you feel the fear.

Step 3: Focus your attention on the fear itself as **consciousness**.

Step 4: Notice you are the observer.

Step 5: Experience the observer and the emotion as made of the same **consciousness**.

Step 6: Let your eyes open and experience objects in the room, i.e., tables, walls, chairs, etc., as being made of the same **consciousness** as the observer who is observing the emotion.

This exercise uplevels this process because you are being asked to experience everything as **consciousness**. In order to experiment further, look at objects in the room as **consciousness** first. In other words, see objects in the room as **consciousness** *first,* then as the object you call table, chair, wall, etc. Next, see everything in the *world as you walk around as being made of the same consciousness as the one that is looking at the objects.*

SADNESS

Meditate: *Focus your attention on the emotion rather than on the story of why you feel the emotion; experience the emotion as made of energy.*

In this meditation you shift your experience of sadness into an experience of energy. We are starting out with the less pleasurable feelings. As time goes on, we'll move to the more pleasurable. For this meditation we'll begin to recall some past situation in which you experienced sadness. If you can't conjure up sadness, you can use any other emotion which is normally labeled unpleasant. Recall a time you felt sad. Move your attention from the story of why you're sad, or why you're feeling emotional, to the sadness itself as energy.

Sadness, anger or joy is energy in different forms. I know you have reasons why you should be sad, but I want you to move your attention from the story or reasons to focus your attention on the sadness itself. See what happens. See if you can begin to work with the energy.

Practice: To practice, sit for about ten minutes. Start by feeling your body, how it's placed. Watch your breath rising and falling. Next, begin to recall a time associated with sadness. Notice people who are involved in the story, notice where you are in the story. Notice if there are any sounds. Are you inside or outside? Are there any temperature differences?

For a few minutes, begin to allow that emotion to build as you allow it to come into your awareness. Notice the feelings associated with the story. Gently, move your attention from the story, reasons or people in your story, and focus your awareness on the emotion itself. See where the feeling is in your body, or the sensations. Notice its size, color, and whether it has a sound. Focus all of your attention on the emotion rather than on the story of the emotion. Witness the emotion. Keep your attention on the emotion rather than on the story of the emotion.

As you watch the emotion, begin to feel it as energy. See the emotion as energy

and witness the energy. Now, feel your
back pressed against the seat, become
more aware of the room, and very gently,
at your own pace, bring your attention
back and let your eyes open.

After giving this meditation in a class, I once got
this feedback: "I felt it as an energy, and yet I wasn't
very—or maybe I wasn't feeling it as an energy. It
didn't feel very good. I was kind of wanting to do
something." I asked, "So your energy sat there?" He
answered, "I felt as if it was moving, but it wasn't feeling very good."

I said it might not feel good, but to take the label
off of the emotion called, *it wasn't feeling good,* and
then I invited him to go back and continue watching the
emotion as energy, rather than the story of the emotion,
without the intention of getting rid of it. what I would
suggest not to do, in such a situation, is to go in and
try to change the emotion or experience. Watch it as
energy. See what happens. The tendency is that sometimes if it's unpleasant, the emotion gets bigger and
bigger. Gradually, however, it starts shifting. It might
take five or ten minutes, maybe five days or five years
or five seconds.

All these meditations are teaching you to change
your habitual pattern about where you put your attention. Idries Shah, noted Sufi Master, suggests that we
must develop *volitional control* over where we put our
attention.[1] Remember to shift the focus from the story

line to focusing on the emotion itself as energy, whether the emotion is pleasant or unpleasant.

Sadness as Consciousness

Step 1: Recall a time you felt sad.

Step 2: Notice where in your body you feel the sadness.

Step 3: Focus your attention on the sadness itself as made of **consciousness**.

Step 4: Notice you are the observer.

Step 5: Experience the observer and the emotion as the same **consciousness**.

Step 6: Let your eyes open and experience objects in the room, i.e., tables, walls, chairs, etc., as being made of the same **consciousness** as the observer and the emotion.

ANGER

Meditate: *Focus your attention on the emotion rather than on the story of why you feel what you feel; experience the emotion as made of energy.*[2]

This meditation focuses on anger, but if another emotion comes up, you can also use that one.

---

[2]In the trilogy *The Way of the Human,* this is discussed in depth that the Enneagram shows the habitual pattern or way "you" place your attention.

Practice: I'd like you to remember a scene in the past; it could have been last year, it could have been five years ago, it could have been ten years ago. Let the emotion called anger come into your awareness. As you watch this scene in your memory, notice yourself in the memory and look around and notice the other people in the memory. Notice what the feeling is or what the sensations are in your body. Focus on the story. Allow the feeling or the sensations of anger to begin to emerge or come to the surface as you watch the movie in your mind, and notice where it is in your body. Notice its shape or its size.

Begin to focus your awareness on this anger, rather than on the story and reasons why you're angry. *Focus your attention on the anger itself.* As you watch the anger, begin to see it as energy. Notice its size or how it might move or not move. At first, it might get more intense; but as you continue to watch it as energy in a compact form, notice what happens. Continue to focus on the anger, allowing it to do what it does. Keep focusing on that energy. Notice what happens as you do.

When you are ready, very gently bring your awareness back to the room.

A student once reported, "My anger was rectangular, and there were two holes on either side." I replied, "If your anger has a particular shape or color, meditate on that and focus your attention on it. Notice what happens."

Anger as Consciousness

Step 1: Recall a time you felt angry.

Step 2: Notice where in your body you feel the anger.

Step 3: Focus your attention on the anger itself as **consciousness**.

Step 4: Notice that you are the observer.

Step 5: Experience the observer and the emotion as made of the same **consciousness**.

Step 6: Let your eyes open and experience objects in the room, i.e., tables, walls, chairs, etc., as being made of the same **consciousness** as the observer and the emotion.

JEALOUSY

Meditate: *On the emotion rather than on the story as to why you feel what you feel; experience the emotion as made of energy.*

Continue to focus your attention on the emotion rather than on the story of the emotion, i.e., the story, the reasons for your jealousy. First, we'll bring up a story of jealousy. Then you'll move your attention away from the story as to why you feel what you feel, and move your attention to the feeling of jealousy itself. If you don't have any conscious feeling of jealousy, use another emotion. I'd like to remind you, too, that we are planting seeds so that when you are jealous a week from now or two years from now, you'll switch your attention from the story as to why you feel jealous to the jealousy itself. Once the shift happens for you once, I can assure you that it will start a whole chain reaction and a shift in the habitual way you use your attention pattern.

I was really angry with some people about a month and a half ago. A friend reminded me, "why meditate on the people and the situation? why not meditate on the feelings?" I did it and everything disappeared. The tendency is to meditate on the people and the situation and all the reasons you have to feel as you do.

Practice: Let your eyes close. I'd like you to remember a past event in which you felt you had every right to be jealous. Notice who's involved in the memory that you're watching. Notice the temperature, or if you can experience any voices or sounds. Let the film roll. Notice the feelings that arise as you watch the film. Watch the film and the story called jealousy. Notice the sensations.

Very gently move your awareness away from the story. Notice where in your body you experience the feelings called jealousy. *Begin to witness the jealousy as energy in a different form.* If you feel the jealousy, if you feel that emotion, begin again to witness it as energy in a different shape or a different form. See if there is a color or a temperature or a sound to the energy:

View it as energy. Listen to its sound. Watch it. Continue to watch whatever feelings are going on inside you and view them as energy.

Notice if your mind wants to go back to the reasons and the story of why you're feeling what you're feeling. If so, pull your attention back to the feelings you're experiencing inside and experience them as energy. Gently, whenever you're ready, bring your awareness back to the room, and let your eyes open.

Past workshop participants have commented about how hard they found it was to shift attention away from the story and onto the feelings because their mind tells them they are justified in feeling the way they do. Sometimes my workshop participants have felt they got "stuck" at some point in the process. When this happens, I suggest that they continue by meditating on the "stuckness" as made of energy.

Students have often asked me about repressing emotions as opposed to expressing them. There's repressing, which means pushing down or sitting on your jealousy or anger. There's expressing: two opposite sides of the same thing. Then there's transmutation, which is to experience it as energy *without any intention of getting rid of it,* just to see what happens. Generally, at some point the energy shifts as you shift your attention pattern and the energy transmutes itself. I'm not going to say, "Don't feel angry." No. I'd like you to watch the jealousy or the anger, whatever it is, as energy and to shift the chronic habitual attention pattern of your awareness. In other words, we all have habitual patterns of where we place our attention and awareness. This process helps us to shift that pattern.

A student followed up on that idea by asking, "what do I do when I'm beginning to feel anger and other energies, and I don't know what to do with it? It makes me feel…well, something like heat. How do you change it once you're aware and focusing on it?" I told this person *not to change* the emotion or reaction or heat but to watch the heat and focus on it, and notice what happened. Don't go halfway.

All I can tell you is my own experience. I experienced extreme anger a few years ago, and I shifted my attention and experienced it as energy. Within seconds I was in ecstasy. It might take you ten minutes or it might take you ten hours. I'm saying to shift your attention pattern by keeping' your attention on the emotion as energy rather then the story, and see what happens without trying to change the experience. A person at one of my workshops said, "I'm experiencing a wall." I said,

"Focus your attention on the wall as energy."

In the middle of yelling at someone, you might see that there's a certain amount of energy. I'm not giving you a "should." You can do whatever you want with it. If you want to yell at somebody, then yell at them. It doesn't matter to me. One option is to express it, if that's the way you want to go.

Another option is to begin to focus on it as energy and see what happens. After you've yelled at someone, you might feel relieved but not have much energy left. For example, after having an orgasm in sex, you might feel relieved and relaxed, but if you can take the sexual energy and focus your attention on it, then you're in a different place altogether. A student asked me whether focusing on the energy would move it up. "Focus on it," I replied, "and see what happens. Your experience might be totally different from mine. It might get bigger and bigger and bigger and bigger, and then you'll see what happens. when I'm feeling sexual, if I happen to be meditating and then some memory or fantasy comes up about whatever, and I get distracted, I focus on the energy of it, it becomes very intense, and then all of a sudden there is a shift and I'm zoomed right into a deep space, I'm literally catapulted."

Another student said, "When I'm really angry, I don't think. I know I'm angry, but the thought of shifting my attention pattern and doing something about it rather than letting the memory go through my mind for hours and hours doesn't dawn on me." This is a practice. Right now the film is going on and on and on.

Hopefully, two weeks from now it'll only go on and on. And then it'll go on. In other words, it's having a pattern and catching your pattern earlier. Say you always pick the wrong relationships; that's your process. Suddenly, ten years later, you say, "Gee, I did it again." And you pick another relationship and it's five years later. When you pick it up again, it's two years later, then it's one year later. Hopefully, you work it out before you die!

A student brought his experience with the teachings of Gurdjieff of trying to be awake and to observe constantly what one does. "When the feeling of anger or whatever came up," he said, "we'd give it a name like John. When it came up later, we could say, 'Here comes John again.

In Psychosynthesis, that's called naming sub-personalities. "Oh, there's John. John's running his number. There's Fred." There even used to be a therapy called Name Therapy. You can give names to all the different parts of your personality and then watch them do their numbers. Using that technique helps to get some distance on them, but there is another level because *you are not your sub-personalities*. This is another level, but using names is a Psychosynthetic way of working on it. You could draw a picture of it and put it on your wall to get more in touch with it and know when the sub-personalities pop up. Here we are de-labeling and working with the *most basic substance, i.e., energy and then* **consciousness**.

A student said that she had been angry with her office partner and "focused very intensely for about half an hour on the feeling." She asked if that was the same thing as we were trying to do with this meditation. I answered, "Yes, if I get angry while she is talking, I'll meditate on the anger or frustration or whatever is going on with me and then I'll go talk with the person later. Many times when I go to talk with a person after I have processed my emotions about them, I feel very different, very connected to them, and very connected to myself."

Experiencing Jealousy as Consciousness

Step 1: Recall a time you felt jealous.

Step 2: Notice where in your body you feel the jealousy.

Step 3: Focus your attention on the jealousy as **consciousness**.

Step 4: Notice that you are the observer.

Step 5: Experience the observer and the emotion as made of the same **consciousness**.

Step 6: Let your eyes open and experience objects in the room, i.e., tables, walls, chairs, etc., as being made of the same **consciousness** as the observer and the emotion.

SEXUALITY

Meditate: *Focus your attention on the sexual sensations rather than on the story as to why you feel sexual.*

If you have sexual fantasies—I know none of you do, but if you did—and you focus your attention on the sexual fantasy, or on the memory of a person, what happens is that you are always looking outside yourself trying to fulfill the sexual fantasy. So your mind is popping up pictures of a sexual fantasy, in some form or another. More than likely, you won't get too much satisfaction, because you will always be fantasizing about somebody else outside of yourself.

I noticed that during the two years I was celibate, I was going through incredible fantasies. Since the fantasies were still there, so were the bodily reactions, so I had a difficult time for two years. It was a 180° shift from my sexual behavior in the 1960's and 1970's where free sexuality was the rule and everybody slept with everybody. Once I started this practice, it shifted my habitual pattern of the way I focused my awareness on the fantasy of sexuality by placing my attention on the energy itself. Where do I feel it? It's exactly the same as all of the emotional issues, except that now we're going to look at what is normally labeled as a more pleasant one.

Shift your attention away from the fantasy, or away from the movie in your mind, and place your attention on the energy itself. Notice what happens as you start focusing your attention on the sexual feelings as energy. Earlier I mentioned the saying in the *Vijnana Bhairava* which went something like, from the remembrance of what it's like to be touching, pressing, kissing, holding, certain feelings arise inside, certain delightful sensations arise inside. However, since there's nobody there, obviously the sensations come from *inside of you.* This seemed very profound to me at the time, that *it's coming from inside of me, because there's no one there.* In other words, if you're fantasizing, and you have the remembrance of those types of things, it brings about such feelings in your body. Since there's nobody there, say when you're driving down the street, then obviously those feelings *are coming from inside of you.* Therefore, rather than focusing on the fantasy and trying to fulfill it by chasing outside of yourself, begin to shift your attention. This simply means moving your attention off of the fantasy and into the experience itself as energy, rather than seeing it as sexual energy and something to work with. It's energy. It's not good or bad or right or wrong or high or low: It's energy.

I remember saying to Baba Prakashananda that I was having problems with my *second* chakra. Babaji said, "Only one chakra: energy." So it's all energy or **consciousness**; only the mind wants to compartmentalize it into chakras and higher and lower, placing judgment evaluations or giving significance to the *labels* which are placed on energy.

The *Yoga Vasishtha: The Supreme Yoga,* by Swami Venkateshananda, is the story of Prince Ram before he realized he was Lord Ram and enlightened. The book contains questions from Ram to his Guru Vasishtha. For pages Vasishtha is describing to Ram the Kundalini, its awakening, piercing the chakras, purifying the 72,000 Nadis, and so on. After a while Ram says, "Now I understand." Vasishtha asks, "what do you understand?" Ram repeats everything that Vasishtha has told him about kundalini, the chakras, etc. Vasishtha says, 'No, none of that is true." Ram asked, "Why did you tell me that story then?" Vasishtha replied, "It's for the unenlightened to give them a *story* to talk about. None of that exists. *"Everything is **consciousness**: nothing exists outside of **consciousness**. Everything is **consciousness**: nothing exists outside of **consciousness**."* The difference and beauty of Tantric meditation is that it is for people that live in the world. Rather than trying to put your mind someplace else, you're always meditating on *what is.* In this way any feeling or thought or emotion can be used as *fuel to bring you back into a deeper connection to yourself and your humanness.*

Practice: Let your eyes close and get yourself comfortable again.

I'd like you to begin to develop a sexual fantasy. You can start by picking someone that you'd like to be with. Notice what they look like, whether there are any sounds. Watch the sexual fantasy. Notice the temperature, notice if there are any smells or any tastes, any sensations. Let the movie in your mind run for a moment.

Gently, shift your attention from the sexual fantasy to the energy in your body itself. Begin by noticing where in your body you feel that energy, where those sensations and those feelings are. Take off the label of sexual feelings or sensations and put your attention on the feelings as energy: where do you feel it, how do you feel it? Has it a color or a shape or a sound? Fixate your attention on the energy itself. If your attention goes toward the fantasy, bring it down again, and focus your attention and watch the energy. Continue to watch, *with no label* called "sexual energy"; begin to witness, and put your attention on it as energy when you are ready, bring your awareness back to the room.

I asked a class if anyone had been able to move attention from the fantasy to the energy itself and if so, what had happened to the energy? Did it get stronger, get weaker, stay the same? A student commented, "when I breathed the energy would go down and come up." Another said, "There was energy going through my whole body." I asked that student, "So the energy was moving?" He replied, "Yes, when I finally focused on the energy itself."

The purpose of this practice is the same as the others in this series, which is to meditate and learn to shift out of habitual ways we place our attention on the story, and place our attention on the feelings themselves as being made of energy. I ask you to take your attention, which is focused on the fantasy, and move it into the feelings themselves and to begin to view feelings that you have inside yourself as energy. In this way, there is no reason to resist, deny or judge yourself for your experience.

As I mentioned earlier, when I lived in an ashram many of us were celibates. I was a very horny celibate for the first two years. I had a lot of fantasies, and when I put my attention on the fantasies, I'd still get bodily reactions. However, when I shifted my attention from the fantasy and toward the feelings themselves, the energy suddenly started to shift.

Tantric scriptures say that, if at the moment of orgasm, you could become introverted, you would experience *Spanda* (the divine throb). What they did not mention was that if at that moment you could *remember* to become introverted, your energy would go in rather than out, and you would go into a deep "no-state". That's the purpose of this meditation.

Experiencing Sexuality as Consciousness

Step 1: Recall a time you felt sexual.

Step 2: Notice where in your body you feel the sexual energy.

Step 3: Focus your attention on the sexuality itself as **consciousness**.

Step 4: Notice you are the observer.

Step 5: Experience the observer and the sexual energy as being made of the same **consciousness**.

Step 6: Let your eyes open and experience objects in the room, i.e., tables, walls, chairs, etc., as being made of the same **consciousness** as the observer and the sexual feelings.

FOOD

Meditate: *Focus your attention on the delightful sensations around food, rather than on the food itself*
(*Vijnana Bhairava,* Jaideva Singh)

This meditation will plant seeds for you. It's probably the most difficult thing to process. As we go on, you'll be processing your senses, which means that you won't be automatically identified with what your senses experience. Working with food, however, is a very big issue.

The method for this meditation is the same as the others. For example, let's imagine that you're sitting at your desk at work, and all of a sudden, you have a thought that says, "I want chocolate," or whatever your fantasy is. Your mind takes off on that and you react to it. By the way, if you want to lose weight, you can use this meditation when you're hungry, i.e., focus your attention on hunger itself as energy rather than on the food fantasy popping up which causes the hunger, and notice what happens. That's a whole meditation. You can't do it if you're not hungry.

You can use the sensations and joy of a chocolate chip cookie or M&M's or whatever. Take your awareness away from this, and meditate on the sensations.

To paraphrase the *Vijnana Bhairava,* meditate on the delight as energy rather than on the object of delight. If it's sexuality, meditate on the delight, rather than on the object of the delight. If you're having sex with some-body, you're more than likely meditating on the person. Turn your attention away from the person, and toward the delight itself, and see what the experience is.

This can be thought of as meditating on the delight as energy rather than on the object of delight, in this case, food.

With various foods on display before you, choose something that you want to take a bite out of [In this class, I asked the students to bring their favorite food treats to class.] What I want you to do is to take a taste and put it in your mouth, and let your eyes close. You can chew it, but do everything *slowly.* In other words, don't swallow it down and reach for another bite.

Practice: I'd like you to notice now that your eyes are closed. I'd like you to focus your atten-tion on the delight, the delightful feelings, as if they are made of energy rather than a picture you might have in your mind of the object of delight. As you feel and experience the sensations, the delightful feelings, or thoughts, or whatever is asso-ciated with the food you have in your mouth, I'd like you to focus your attention on the delightful sensations, rather than on the object of the delight. See if you can keep your attention on the delight, rather than the object of delight. Experience the delight as energy. Gently, bring your awareness back to the room and let your eyes open.

A student commented, "I've given up cigarettes, I've given up booze, and now I have to give up food?" "No," I told him, "I'm not saying that." Personally, I'm not into that at all. *You don't have to give up anything. You don't have to let go of anything; it's the attachment to it that is to be let go of.* If you eat good food, that's fine; if you eat bad food, that's fine. If you have a glass of wine, that's fine; if you don't, that's fine, too. You have a *choice,* that's all. It doesn't matter to me either way. That's what I'm saying. A friend of mine went to see Nisargadatta Maharaj and asked him, "Should I stay in India or go back to the States?" He replied, "whether you stay in India or go back to the States, *there will be no gain, there will be no loss.*"

Another student summed up his reactions with, "It feels like one of the real heavy problem areas." I said, "Yes, it's a much deeper fusion or identification than sex." I would have thought the bottom line was sex, but when I didn't have food, in India, I went *crazy.* I had no choice of my own when I had to process food. I had no choice because in India at times there was no food.

Experience the Desire for Food as Consciousness

Step 1: Recall a time you had a desire or fantasy for food.

Step 2: Notice where in your body you felt the food desire or fantasy.

Step 3: Focus your attention on the energy or desire for food or the hunger as **consciousness.**

Step 4: Notice that you are the observer of that **consciousness.**

Step 5: Experience the observer and the emotion as the same **consciousness.**

Step 6: Let your eyes open and experience objects in the room, i.e., tables, walls, chairs, etc., as being made of the same **consciousness** as the observer and the sensation of hunger for food.

JOY

Meditate: *Find the source of your joy.*

I want to include this meditation because the mind fantasizes about joyful experiences, and so rather than get caught up in trying to fulfill these fantasies and then feeling frustrated when you don't, you can begin to find that the joy comes from inside of you.

Practice: Notice where and how you are sitting and recall a very joyful fantasy or experience. Let your mind find that place. As it begins to happen, notice the joyful feelings inside of yourself. However, instead of watching a little you in the memory experiencing that joy, imagine unzipping the skin of that little person in the memory and stepping inside so that you right now are experiencing the joy. Find the space from which that joy arises. Find the source of that joy. Whenever you're ready, bring your awareness back to the room, let your eyes open.

Here is a student comment: "when I went from the experience to the place inside, I found it in my heart; it was like light. I had trouble sustaining that—it would diminish, then expand, so I found that when I inhaled, I could control it and make it larger. It was as if I was playing with that, but I couldn't sustain it."

I asked him, "Were you able to find the space beyond that?" He said that he had tried to make it happen. I said that I understood. "How do you get beyond that?" he asked.

I told him, "You trace it back."

He said, "How? Because the breath seems to be such a powerful influence. I remember one time in a meditation workshop wishing I could stop breathing so I could find the space!"

"Yes," I replied, "unless you begin to focus on the witness of the breathing. Who is watching the joy? Your experience was that the joy comes and goes. You were trying to control it. who is it that is witnessing not only the coming and going of the joy but the attempt to control its comings and goings?"

Another student said, "I must have been in a masochistic mood. when you suggested the meditation, I had images of many joyful times in my past, but, when I entered the meditation, my memory was of a beautiful spring day when I was flying a kite with a woman I really cared about and her little daughter. It was the worst relationship I ever had! It was truly the most masochistic thing that I ever let happen to myself, but that was probably the best day of the relationship. That's the way the meditation went, and I never did get down inside myself."

I told him, "I think if you play with these meditations, you will find that the space where joy arises and the space where grief arises is the same. They are not different spaces.

The student continued, "That's interesting. My memory was a combination of joy and grief."

Pleasure and pain ultimately become the same because they come from the same space, and they are made of the same substance.

Experiencing Joy as Consciousness

Step 1: Recall a time you felt joy.
Step 2: Notice where in your body you feel the joy.
Step 3: Focus your attention on the joy itself as **consciousness**.
Step 4: Notice that you are the observer.

Step 5: Experience the observer and the emotion as made of the same **consciousness**.

Step 6: Let your eyes open and experience objects in the room, i.e., tables, walls, chairs, etc., as being made of the same **consciousness** as the observer and the emotion.

CHAKRAS

4 / CHAKRAS

As mentioned earlier, chakras are made of **con-sciousness**. I think, however, it is important to at least explore some chakra meditations.

The chakras are subtle energy centers, the major ones running along the spinal column. Actually, the word "chakra" means spinning wheel. For our purposes, however, we will think of them as localized energy only.

How does the Indian system of the yoga of liberation apply to Western psychotherapy? Clearly, the root, or first, chakra deals with survival issues (life and death). At this level the symbol of the snake wrapped three and one-half times with its tail in its mouth would symbolize the futility of this life experience. The second chakra (four fingers below the navel), often associated with sexuality; can best be exemplified by Freudian psychotherapy, or Reichian therapy.

The third chakra, associated with power, lies at the pit of the stomach or solar plexus. This chakra is often associated with most of the power therapies promoted by the human potential movement, such as Gestalt, i.e., the "be-powerful" therapies.

The heart chakra is located at the center of the chest; the place of unconditional love is at this chakra. This is the plane where the beingness within oneself is seen as the same as within others. This generates an uninterrupted experience of unconditional love. It is beyond mind, just pure being. To sit in the heart requires a letting go of traditional psychotherapy, for at the heart there is justness and an "isness" or I AM, a coming together of the pairs of opposites. In the heart, the movement is toward unity **consciousness** rather than an experience of separation from them and us, to just US.

Although the throat chakra represents creation, the third eye is the turning within, whereby the world is seen as a projection of one's own **consciousness**.

The crown chakra is the final threshold wherein the ONE becomes many, and the many merges back into the ONE.

Meditate: *Imagine there is a thin tube that runs from the base of the spine to the crown of the head.*

(Vijnana Bhairava, Jaideva Singh)

Meditate on the void inside that tube.

There are many, many energy centers in the body, but only seven are major ones. We're going to be using the major chakras only. The first one is at the base of the spine and goes up the spine. The second one is about four fingers below the navel. The third is in the solar plexus area. The fourth is in the heart, the fifth is in the throat, the sixth is the third eye, and the seventh is in the crown of the head.

Practice: I would like you to imagine that there is a thin tube running from the base of your spine all the way up to the crown of your head right in the center of your spine. Focus your attention on that for now. Notice what the tube looks like and what it feels like. Notice if there is any sound coming from inside the tube. Turn your attention to the void inside the tube, and focus attention on that space for about ten minutes. Meditate on the space or void inside the tube. Now, gently, bring your awareness back to the room, and let your eyes open.

The Heart Chakra

Meditate: 1. That your physical heart is the heart of an enlightened being.
2. That everyone's heart is the heart of an enlightened being.

This is a group meditation. Think about someone you believe is an enlightened being, i.e., Jesus, Buddha, Krishna, whoever.

Practice: This meditation can be done in a group as well as alone.

Let your eyes close. I'd like you to very gently focus your attention on your physical heart. Feel your heart beating, feel it and see it, get a good deep sense of the beating of your physical heart, and listen or feel or see your physical heart beating. Let it exaggerate itself so that you really feel it or hear it or see it. Keep your attention on your physical heart, feeling or hearing or seeing it pumping. I'd like you to imagine that inside your chest is actually beating the physical heart of an enlightened being, that her or his physical heart is beating inside your body. Feel his or her heart pumping, hear it pumping. Feel the beating of their heart inside your body, the blood rushing through the veins. Feel all the energy of this realized being's heart inside your body.

Imagine that inside every person's chest beats the heart of an enlightened being. In a moment, I'm going to ask you to open your eyes and make eye contact with someone in the room, realizing that their heart and your heart are the hearts of enlightened beings. Okay, let your eyes open. Now make eye contact with a person, keeping that awareness. Keep your attention focused on your heart as the heart of an enlightened being. Make eye contact with someone and imagine that their heart and your heart are the hearts of enlightened beings. Focus on your own heart and let it flow out. One after another, make eye contact with several people in the group. Make eye contact with someone else. Make eye contact with someone else. Now with someone else. Make eye contact with someone else. Feel your own heartbeat as the heartbeat of an enlightened being and know that theirs is the same.

A student observed after this meditation, "It makes you wonder if inside, we all know we are enlightened. I couldn't always see eyes, but I was feeling the energy at some level." I told him that this had happened to me years before, when I was walking down the street in Los Angeles. I didn't even know it was a formal meditation. It just happened spontaneously.

Another student commented, "While you were talking about having us picturing our heart as that of an enlightened being, all humanity became—all the hearts started to connect. I went through the heart of one person, and it was all one big heart! When I came out of the meditation, I could see light around everyone.

Another student said, "The women all looked like madonnas," and another said, "That plant was putting out light, especially one leaf." Someone asked me how you can bring this into the world. I suggested that if you can change your focus to seeing everyone's heart as the heart of an enlightened being, it will transform your experience. When Swami Muktananda gave his talks, he used to say, "I welcome you all with all of my heart. People think that I'm saying this to butter you up, but actually this is my experience. To welcome another person with love, to see God inside of them is the highest practice."

We must understand that this is an internal practice; it is not about behaving outwardly or acting like a guru. It's not about imitating someone. I saw many people around Swami Muktananda trying to imitate the way he walked, his mannerisms and so on, but it had nothing to do with who he was, nothing to do with the state of an enlightened heart. I've seen many who have started taking on the personality of a saint, rather than that inner essence. I've seen a lot of people in ashrams sell out their integrity. They start acting like they imagine they should, even though it doesn't *fit* them. That's a nice meditation; it's always been a favorite.

Meditate: *Mentally enter into the cave of your heart.*

Practice: Feel your body, how it's situated, and your breath, and notice your muscles. Now I'd like you to imagine that in the center of your chest, in your heart, there is a cave, the cave of your heart, and for the next few minutes, I would like you to enter into the cave of your heart, in the center of your chest. And rather than imagining a small you entering into the cave of your heart, crawl into the skin of that small you, so that you enter into the cave of your heart from behind your own eyes. As you enter the cave, go down deeper and deeper.

Meditate: *Merge your heart and mind.*

Practice: Let your eyes close again. First, I'd like you to let an image come to you of your heart. Notice what your heart looks like, what it feels like; it might even be a sound. And now allow yourself to actually climb inside your heart so that you are actually there inside your heart, rather than simply seeing a small you in front of you going inside your heart. I'd like you to actually be inside your heart. Notice what it's like to be in your heart. Gently, step out of your heart so that you're watching it from a distance. I'd like you to imagine it as if from a distance, then put brackets around

it and move it off to the side for a moment.
Next, develop an image or let an image
come to you, of your mind, and see it from
a distance. Notice what it looks like, its
texture, what it feels like. It might even
have particular sounds. Let yourself step
into the picture so that you are actually
inside your mind, then let yourself step
outside your mind again so that you're
watching it from a distance. Now, split
the movie screen in your mind, so that
on one side of the movie screen is your
heart and on the other side is your mind.
Watch them from a distance. Each has its
particular function: both are very functional. Now, let the two images become
one image, so that the heart and the mind
become one. Notice what it looks like,
maybe the sounds, the feeling of the heart
and the mind becoming one. Now, let
yourself *step into* this newly merged heart
and mind; let yourself step into the image
so that you're actually inside the two of
them that are now merged into one. And
allow yourself to feel the feeling and
experience the sounds, the feeling, all of
the sensations of being there inside. And
becoming aware of your body, where it's
sitting, and your breath, very gently come
back to the room, and let your eyes open.

THE BODY

5 / THE BODY

Much has been written about the over identification of the self with the body. In India it is said that meditations that enable an individual to dis-identify with their body helps toward developing inner freedom. In Kashmir Shaivism, and Vedanta, *"I am not the body!"* is proclaimed again and again. In the *Bhagavad Gita,* Krishna teaches Ariuna that there *is* a body.

Krishna calls the body the field, because the seeds of action are sown there, and it is in the field or body that the fruits of our actions are reaped (what you sow, so shall you reap). Krishna further teaches to *know the knower of the field* (the witness). This is not the context to discuss other points of view. For now, let us look at the Indian point of view. In my forthcoming book, *The Way of the Human,* the body is the pathway in what I call *biological spirituality,* which leads us to the underlying unity or Quantum Consciousness.

In the *Shiva Sutras* it reads, "The Body is the Offering." More easily understood is that the body can be viewed from the point of view of the inner witness, and that experiences can be experienced as originating with, or as a reflection of, that witness.

The following meditations will help you to experience these understandings.

Contemplate: *Without using your thoughts, memory, emotions, associations or perceptions —What is it that lifts the legs, moves the arms and hears?*

I really like this meditation; it is very fast but very powerful. Half of it is done with open eyes and half with eyes closed. Sit for about fifteen minutes.

Practice: Let your eyes close once again as you go back into that space inside yourself. Begin to notice what happens when, without using your thoughts, memory, emotions, associations, perceptions, attention or intensions, "What is it that lifts the arms, moves the legs, and hears? What is it that lifts the arms, moves the legs, and hears?" As you begin to uncover the various layers, notice "Who" is it or what is it that lifts the arms, moves the legs, and hears? Whenever you're ready, feel your body pressed against the chair or seat, notice your breathing, and begin to bring your awareness back to the room. One student said, "Without using my memory, mind or associations, there was nothing there; so I guess *nothing* lifts the legs, moves the arms and hears."

Meditate: *Imagine yourself being breathed rather than breathing.*

Practice: Feel your body pressed and supported. Watch your breath. What I want you to do with your breath is to speed it up a little bit. Now I'd like you to slow it down a little. Now go back to your regular breathing and experience yourself breathing as you usually do. Now, I'd like you to experience, however you can, *being breathed.* I'll say it again: Experience *being breathed,* rather than breathing—be *breathed.* All you have to do is let it happen and it will happen. *Be breathed.* And, very gently, in your own time, bring your awareness back to the room and let your eyes gently open.

One student said in reaction. "It was as if there was only the breather and no thing that was being breathed." Another student said, "I felt a power or a force beyond me breathing me rather than me breathing—it was quite blissful."

Contemplate: *The senses move not by my will, but by the will of the void or emptiness.*

I'd like you to contemplate the five senses. Senses are moved by the will of the void or emptiness, *not by your will.* If your eyes move a certain way, it's the will of the void; it's not your will. I want you to contemplate that the senses move not by your will, but by the will of the void, which is the will of the divine. Everything moves by the will of the void or the divine. Contemplate that for a minute. Nisargadatta Maharaj used to say to *allow the void to live you or through you.*

Contemplate: *That you are not living a life, but that you are being lived. That the void lives through you and it is the void's life, not yours.*

A student comment about this meditation: "What it did more than anything was make me realize that the 'I' that thinks it's doing all of this is my own creation, it's an illusion. It's always the divine or void that's moving everything, and to superimpose on that another belief that 'I'm doing it' is the ego and illusion." I told him that one of the first principles of yoga is, "I am not the doer." I will add to that, "The void does everything." He replied, "I'll think about that. It makes the 'I' a real illusion." Not doing anything—that's a real letting go, because the 'I' wants to control. "It's the old saying: 'There but for the grace of God (the void) go I.'" It's the awareness that the void creates the mind by becoming solid, by condensing down and becoming thoughts, objects, and ideas, and ultimately, to see your mind and everything else as being *made* by the void and as the same substance *as* the void.

Meditate: *On the lightning—like energy moving from the root chakra to the crown of your head.*

                                    (Vijnana Bhairava, Jaideva Singh)

Practice: Let your eyes close again, feel your body pressed against the seat, and notice your breath again. Starting with the root chakra at the base of the spine—I'd like you to imagine a lightning—like energy moving from the base of the spine, piercing all the chakras all the way up to the crown of the head, like a bolt of lightning. Again experience a lightning—like energy; like a lightning bolt, moving from the base of the spine to the crown of the head like a bolt of lightning or a clap of thunder. You might even smell as well as envision or feel a lightning—like energy moving up the base of the spine to the crown of the head. Like a flash of lightning. Gently, feeling your back pressed against the seat, let your eyes open.

Some students have reported that this meditation made their skin tingle. One student commented, "I heard thunder." Another commented, "I found, with a couple of the other meditations, I heard thunder and lightning and the whole thing. I don't feel it; I hear it." Another commented, "I've heard thunder with the third eye meditation, and there's a smell that goes with the lightning one.

Meditate: *On the energy moving up from the root chakra to the crown of your head like rays of the sun, getting more and more subtle as it reaches the crown of your head.*
(Vijnana Bhairava, Jaideva Singh)

Feel your body pressed against the couch or chair or floor, wherever you are. Notice your breath, allowing it to slow down. Start with the root at the base of your spine, and imagine that there is energy; the metaphor is that this energy is like the rays of the sun coming from the root chakra, going upward to the crown of your head, getting more and more subtle. Meditate on the energy, beginning at the root chakra, piercing all of the chakras on the spine. Like rays of the sun, the energy becomes more and more subtle as it goes toward and reaches the crown of the head. Allow the energy that you see or feel or even hear and notice how the rays of the sun are getting more and more subtle, eventually dissolving. Let them dissolve at the crown of your head, getting more and more subtle, beginning with the root chakra, moving upward until the rays of the sun dissolve at the crown of your head. Gently, bring your awareness back to the room. When you're ready, let your eyes flutter open.

A student commented, "It was hard. My mind even started wandering, because, although I could imagine the crown of my head really well and the energy sort of dissipated, I couldn't experience a vast sun—like energy coming up. The best I could do was try to visualize a little." I asked this student if she could feel the energy, and she answered that she could feel it a little on her head.

Meditate: 1. Meditate on your physical body as if it had no support.
2. Meditate on the universe as your body.
(Vijnana Bhairava, Jaideva Singh)

Practice: I want you to notice where you are sitting and how you are sitting, where your body is right now, and I'd like you to meditate on, or focus your attention on, or imagine that your body is without physical support. I'd like you to imagine that *your body is without physical support.* Then, for a moment I'd like you to let go of that and to watch your breath. Watch your breath rising and falling.

In this meditation, we are going to begin to include everything as part of us. So as you focus on your physical body, very gently allow everything in the room, imagine that everything in the room is your physical body, every person, every thing. Expand so that everything in the room is part of your physical body. Stretch your awareness to include everything in the room. Let everything in the room be part of your physical body, part of your awareness. Then, very gently I'd like you to include the apartment complex that you live in. Let your awareness stretch, expand, to include your apartment complex as part of your physical body. Then expand to include your neighborhood. Include all that in your awareness as part of your physical body. Notice that at first there might be a little resistance, but expand gently to include the entire neighborhood in your awareness as part of your physical body. Gently expand to include all of your city so that it's all inside your awareness as part of your physical body. Gently include your city and the surrounding ones in your awareness as part of your physical body. Let your awareness spread to include the whole state as part of your physical body. Let your awareness expand to include neighboring states as part of your physical body. Let your awareness expand until your awareness includes your country. Imagine that you can expand to include all of that inside your awareness as part of your physical body. Now see if you can include the entire Northern hemisphere inside your awareness as part of your physical body. Gently expand to include it. Then include South America as part of your physical body. Include the oceans on both sides, Atlantic and Pacific, as part of your physical body. Include Asia and India and Southeast Asia. Include it. Africa. Europe. Keep expanding so you include the whole planet inside your awareness as part of your physical body. Very gently, whenever you are ready, bring your attention back to the room. Let your eyes open.

One student said she had a funny reaction when I said to imagine there was no support for the body: "I was extremely aware of the chair. The chair was there, but the body wasn't. I couldn't feel my body, but I could feel the chair. All of a sudden there was the chair and nobody in it, so it was really easy to expand and bring in the other things." Another student said, "I felt myself leaning back and zooming around in the universe. Then when we switched to including things in our awareness and hit Albuquerque, I was lost in the sense of freedom and never recovered."

A third student had this comment about losing a sense of the body: "The part where you sort of erase your body—what I was doing then was visualizing that I had a little string that I unravel. I unravel the string and the body disappears. This time I got up to the point where I had the top of my head left. Then I started to float in the water and it started to float down the stream; then I got out of that and you started to get into where I was supposed to include everything." A fourth said he had a little trouble getting Asia in along with North and South America because he had trouble looking around the planet.

Meditate: *On your skin as if it is a wall.*

Contemplate: *There is nothing substantial inside it.*
                    (Vijnana Bhairava, Jaideva Singh)

This is a very simple meditation, and as time goes on, you'll see that you will need explanations less and less.

Practice: Again, let your eyes close. What I'd like you to do is to focus your attention on your skin boundary, your physical skin boundary. I'd like you to focus your attention on your skin as though it were a wall, as though it were a physical wall. As you focus your attention on your skin as though it were a wall, notice its texture, what it's made out of. Notice how it feels and looks. And now, I'd like you to contemplate that there is nothing substantial inside it. As you feel the wall and see how it looks, contemplate that there's nothing substantial inside it. Continue to contemplate, "There is nothing substantial inside it." Very gently, bring your awareness back to the room.

Contemplate: 1. *Experience your body as made of* **consciousness**.
2. *The possibility that every person is made of* **consciousness**.
3. *The possibility that all objects are made of* **consciousness**.

These three meditations can be done alone or in a group session.

Practice: Now we're going to be working on seeing our body as **consciousness**. I'd like you to sit for about 20 minutes and then another few minutes with eyes open. So again, find a quiet space inside yourself. In this meditation, imagine that your body is made of **consciousness**. The way to do that is to allow your body to be made of energy or **consciousness** *in one sweep,* rather than doing it piece by piece—in one sweep, holding the energy and the feeling. Maybe even the sound of the body as **consciousness**. In one sweep, experience your body as energy or **consciousness**. What does your body look like? What is it feeling? What sounds do you hear when your whole body is **consciousness**? Continue experiencing your body in one sweep, being made of **consciousness**.

Now contemplate that the same that is in your body is in other bodies and that all bodies are made of the same **consciousness**. Finally, contemplate that all objects or things in the world are made of **consciousness**, appearing in different shapes or forms. Last, very gently, let your eyes open, making eye contact with other people in the room, imagining that their bodies and your body are made of the same substance, the same energy or **consciousness**. Continue to make eye contact with other people in the room in the same way.

THE SENSES

6 / THE SENSES

The senses—seeing, feeling, hearing, tasting, smelling—operate on their own. What is important to discern is the EMPTINESS, or *Isness,* just behind the senses. As that is discovered, the meditations can be viewed as processes or ways in which "beliefs" about the senses and the body can be brought up and worked with. It should be mentioned that it is the EMPTINESS which moves the witness, that moves the senses and creates their reactions.

In the *Bhagavad Gita,* Krishna (Emptiness) drives the chariot (the body) powered by the horses (the senses).

Following are meditations designed to release you from sense reactions placed on automatic.

VISUALIZATION

Meditate: 1. Imagine that your body is on fire. It begins in your right toe and moves up until your whole body is in flames.

(Vijnana Bhairava, Jaideva Singh)

2. Imagine the fire spreading until the whole world is on fire.
3. Imagine that there is a thumb-sized, wickless flame in the center of your chest.
4. Imagine that there is a third eye in the center of your chest.
5. Imagine that there is a third eye in the crown of your head.

Practice: I'd like you to feel the way in which you're sitting. Notice how your hands are. Notice your breath. Notice any sounds that are around you as you begin. Then I'd like you to imagine that there is a fire in your right big toe and that it is beginning to spread. It goes up your leg, and into your other leg, through your body until your experience is that your body is on fire. I'd like you to notice if there's a temperature change with these sensations. As you see your body on fire, notice if there are any sounds in the background or any smells. Hold the experience of your entire body bursting into flames. Notice the fire; your entire body is on fire. Notice the temperature change and the sensations. Notice if there are any sounds of burning, or any smells as you continue to experience your body *bursting into flames.*

The fire begins to spread to the floor where you're sitting; it's beginning to *burst into flames,* and then the entire room. It's beginning to spread to the entire building, all the way down your street, in all directions. The entire city has *burst into flames.* Notice if there's any temperature change, smells, or sounds. The fire has spread to envelop your entire state; it has *burst into flames.* The fire has spread to your neighboring states, and they all *burst into flames.* Imagine the entire world, so that everything in the entire world is on fire. Notice if there are any smells or sounds.

Now begin to bring the fire backwards so that the fire begins to get smaller and smaller, until eventually only your body is in flames. Then imagine the flame getting still smaller and smaller, until it sits as a thumb-sized wickless flame in the center of your chest. Imagine that there is a wickless flame in the center of your chest. Notice the temperature change, the smells, the sounds. Now imagine the thumb-sized, wickless flame is in your third eye. Next, allow the crown of your head to have a thumb-sized, wickless flame which ignites and burst into flames.

Very gently, whenever you're ready to bring your awareness back into the room, let your eyes gently open.

SOUND

Meditate: *Find the empty space or void at the end of a sound.*

(*Vijnana Bhairava,* Jaideva Singh)

In this meditation, pluck the string of any stringed instrument, and follow the sound. Sit for about ten minutes for the next two meditations.

Practice: Let yourself go into a quiet place, and consider that this meditation is about sound. Often when we are meditating, sound can knock us out of that state, so the next two meditations are about utilizing sound. Have a friend pluck the string of a guitar or a similar instrument while you meditate. Follow the sound of the string and find the void or the empty space at the end of the sound. If you hear a voice, find the space at the end of each word. If it's a voice inside your head, find the space at the end of that voice. Follow the sound, and find the space or the void at the end of the sound. Find the space or the void at the end of the sound. Glide into the space or the void at the end of the. sound. Then stay in the void at the end of the sound. Now, stay and go very deeply into the next space at the end of the sound. If you hear a sound external to your meditation, find the space at the end of that sound. Whether the sounds are internal, like your own voice inside your head, or external like some random sound, find the space at the end of the sound. Now stay in the space at the end of the occurrence of any sound. Feel your body, how you're seated, noticing your breath. Begin to bring your awareness back to the room. Whenever you're ready, taking your time, let your eyes open.

Meditate: *On the space at the end of a sound.*

Here is a meditation that continues from the last one. We are working with being able to utilize sounds that we hear in meditation, so these meditations can be very valuable. In this meditation, then, whether you hear a voice, a plane going overhead, traffic sounds, or a voice inside your head, I want you to find the space at the end of the sound. If you're listening to a sentence in your mind or to an idea, to find the space at the end of the sound.

You're going to drop into that space, that
silence, that void.

Practice: Let yourself drop into a quiet space and
begin by experiencing the space or the
void after the occurrence of a sound, of
the word, or an idea, or any sound. Use
every sound either inside or outside yourself and find the space at the end of it. Sink
deeply into that space. Whenever you're
ready, bring your awareness back to the
room; notice your breathing and let your
eyes open.

OPEN-EYED MEDITATIONS

Meditate: *Look at an object in the room; then withdraw your energy from it, eliminating the
knowledge of the object along with the
thought or impression.*
(Vijnana Bhairava, Jaideva Singh)

The last two meditations in this chapter are open-
eyed. The first one involves practice with objects in the
room. When you try this meditation, you might want to
practice with a small group, since I'd like you to make
eye-contact with a partner, then switch in the middle to
another partner.

Practice: First, pick an object in the room. Now I'd like you to begin to pull back your attention, or your energy. In other words, your energy is going out, and it's very subtle, toward a particular object, like the couch, for instance. Pull your attention or your energy back inside. As you look at an object, pull your energy back, past the point of having the impression or knowledge. of the impression. Pull it back to a place where the object is still there, but you're looking from the EMPTINESS. Look at an object in the room right now and slowly withdraw your energy from it, past the knowledge of the object, along with the thought or the impression.

A student commented that she could get beyond the knowledge of the object except for its color. I said that, "You will continue to see the color, but it will no longer register as, say, the rug in the living room. In other words, the color—is still there, and it's not going to disappear, but you're moving, withdrawing your attention prior to the thought and impression, even the knowledge of it. *It is a very deep focus.*"

I'd like you to pair up with a partner for this next practice.

Practice: Let your eyes close for a second, then make eye contact with your partner. Let your energy withdraw, removing any knowledge or information or any impressions or thoughts you have about that person. Turn your energy inside, withdrawing it backward. Withdraw your energy. Let your eyes close again. Make eye contact with another person, and again gently withdraw your energy, removing any thoughts or impressions or information you have about that person. Find the space before any thought information; withdraw your energy backwards to that point. Continue to withdraw your energy backwards.

A student reacted: "Everything went out of focus, and my partners began to become less solid. It was really interesting because what I noticed was the more I looked from *back there,* the less solid she became and that there was this great big light around everything and then the moment of complete detachment comes."

Another student commented, "The focusing happened very fast for me. Suddenly I was oscillating back and forth, and I was focusing very fast." In response to this student, I said, "The deep focusing is what happens. Everything loses its form because we make a form like a chair solid by the concepts in our mind. Then, if you pull your attention or energy back, it loses its *solidness,* since everything is made out of energy, and you are moving and looking from beyond your belief structures, which give solid structure to objects, people and events."

This is a good meditation to use if you're in a relationship with somebody, and you're in the middle of a heated discussion. If you can remember to do this meditation with them, you have to drop all of your concepts about how right you are and move past any impressions or information or any knowledge you have about that other person. This meditation will begin to dissolve everything, because you move into a space where none of your structures and identities exist.

This meditation works because once you start training yourself to do it, you're doing it *all* of the time, seeing and experiencing that everything is "energy" or **consciousness** as you look from *back there.* In this way, each moment can be experienced *right now, in present time,* rather than experiencing the present in terms of the *past* explanations you created about the present.

A student commented, "I felt as if nobody was there, so it feels as if you really end up with nothing. All of a sudden, my partner wasn't there." I asked this student if she was here. She said, "No, I was getting lost, too." I said you sound "like being a drop in the ocean complaining it was not part of the ocean.

She answered, "Well, then the ocean doesn't exist either. It becomes—it's not pleasurable. That's why I don't think I have found the truth yet. Rather than you become everything or you're a part of everything, it's as if everything becomes nothing. I am wondering why I would seek that."

I commented, "You can begin to withdraw your attention from any object, thereby getting your power back. Turn your energy back toward yourself In other words, everything in the world has power (energy) and what you can do is withdraw your energy from all people, situations, and objects, so that you have your power (energy) back instead of it being outside of you. For example, it's a matter of reabsorbing your own "energy" or **consciousness**, or in a Tibetan or Jungian sense, owning everything as a projection of your own **consciousness**.

"I guess what I'm saying," she continued, "is that I didn't feel that I was getting more power. I felt everything was fading, including myself. So are you saying that you can pull energy out so that other things have less power and you have more?"

I said, "At one level you can get' more power, and at the next level there is nothing, neither *you* nor *it* to get power from. Therefore, it becomes a non-issue."

I asked her to do the meditation again with me. I said, "Withdraw your energy as you breathe and look at me; do you begin to disappear? What happened?" She said, "I guess constantly seeking meaning, and what this meditation does is *strip* anything of meaning."

I pointed out to her, "When you say meaning, what you are really saying is that you want things to have meaning in life—meaning and purpose. That's the nature of the mind. The mind is not you. It's the nature of the mind to seek meaning and purpose. I'm not saying that you shouldn't look for meaning, but let your mind do it. You're watching. If you jump in there, and try to figure it out, you'll get burned out. I'm saying let your mind do whatever it does, and I would never say that you shouldn't." She said, "I guess I'm looking for a state of peace or happiness." I repeated what Nisargadatta Maharaj said when someone stated:

"I want to be happy." He said, "That's nonsense. Happiness is-where the *'I'* isn't."

Meditate: *Imagine that the world is a magician's trick or the jugglery of a juggler.*
                      (Vijnana Bhairava, Jaideva Singh)

Here is another open-eyed meditation, although it begins with eyes closed. You are going to think about a particular way of viewing the world, then open your eyes and view it that way.

Practice: Close your eyes for a few minutes and contemplate that the world is like something produced by a juggler in a circus, and that everything is being constantly juggled very spontaneously, almost like a magician's trick and that somehow everyone and everything landed this way. Let your mind expand to experience that the world is like jugglery, a magician's trick. Somehow, it all landed here, and everybody somehow lands wherever they land. Now, open your eyes and look around the room, and see if you can imagine that everything has been juggled somehow like a magician's trick.

In 1984 I visited with Satya Sai Baba in India, and experienced seeing the world as a magic trick, almost as if the world had sprung spontaneously out of a puff of smoke from his hand.

Meditate: 1. Letting your eyes move from object to object, find the empty space between two objects.

For the first part, let your eyes move, eyes open, from object to object in the room, very quickly. Find the empty space between two objects. As you focus on one object and then another, there is a space. Find the empty space or *gap* between two objects.

2. Letting your eyes open and close, imagine the world appearing and disappearing.

For the second part, let your eyes close for a second, and imagine that when your eyes are closed, as they're closed now, that the world disappears. And when your eyes open, the world obviously appears. To expand this a little, when your eyes close, the world is *destroyed* or disappears—destroyed is a hard word to hear—and when your eyes open, the world is created, or *appears.*

Practice: For a few seconds, let your eyes open, and imagine the world being created. Now, let your eyes close, and imagine the world being destroyed. Let your eyes be open, and the world will appear. Let your eyes close, and imagine the world disappears. And open, and it appears; closed, and it disappears. Open, and it is created; closed, and it is destroyed. And open, and it appears, closed, and it disappears. Very gently, begin to feel your body pressed and supported, and notice your breath. Allow your breath to come a little bit into your chest. Become aware of the room around you and, whenever you re ready to come back to the room, let your eyes open.

Meditate: *Withdraw all your senses into the void in the center of your chest.*

Practice: Feel your body again, however it is supported, and notice your breathing again.

To start this meditation, first find the void in the center of your chest. Next, enter into that void in the center of your chest. Imagine that you can sit looking out from the void in the center of your chest. From that position, I would like for you to withdraw all of your senses: touch, smell, taste, sound, even sight. See if you can withdraw all of your senses, for a moment, into that void in the center of your chest. Move all of your attention there. And now, beginning with the sense of touch, withdraw the energy from the sense of touch, and begin to move it into the void in the center of your chest. Focus your attention on the sense of touch and withdraw your energy from the sense of touch. Use that energy and bring it into the void at the center of your chest. Just imagine it withdrawing, going inside in the direction of the void in the center of your chest.

Now move to the sense of taste. Notice how your energy is involved in the sense of taste, and withdraw the energy from the sense of taste, and move it, or allow it to go, into the void at the center of your chest. Imagine it, feel it or see it moving, into the void at the center of your chest.

Now move to the sense of smell. Again, withdraw the energy, the attention, of the sense of smell, and allow the energy to move into the void at the center of your chest. Keep withdrawing the energy of your sense of smell into the void at the center of your chest. Now move to the sense of hearing or sound. Withdraw your energy from the sense of sound into the void and move that energy into the void in the center of your chest. Let the energy involved in the sense of sound withdraw itself into the void in the center of your chest. Now, notice the attention of the energy in the sense of sight, and again, withdraw the energy involved in the sense of sight, and allow it to go into the void in the center of your chest. Allow all of the energy to withdraw from the sense of sight, and move it to the void in the center of your chest. And now, starting back again with the sense of touch, focus your attention on the void before the sense of touch. Focus your attention on the void before the sense of taste. Focus on the void before the sense of smell. Focus on the void before the sense of hearing. And now, meditate on the void before the sense of hearing. And, finally, focus on the void before the sense of sight.

Gently, feel your body, wherever it's sitting, and notice your breathing. Whenever you're ready, let your eyes open, and come back to the room.

A student's comment: "That was very intense.

When I started withdrawing my senses, heat started building up in my body, and I found the temperature rising. When I got to withdrawing vision, I realized that it wasn't dark when I withdrew it, that there was a lot of light. I always thought the void had to be darkness, without any energy. There seemed to be tremendous power. It is interesting because there is so much energy involved *'out there.'*' A teacher of mine in India used to say, "Stay in-drawn; keep your attention inside, rather than being drawn out by the senses to objects outside of yourself."

THE MIND

7 / THE MIND

Philosophers, psychologists, doctors, social workers, self-explorers and yogis have pondered the nature of the mind and its contents. To the psychologist or Western self-explorer, the mind is made of thoughts, ideas, and patterns generally created during a person's childhood. The handling of the mind can vary from analysis to body work, hypnosis to emotional release. What is clear is that from a Western point of view, the mind *needs to be handled.*

From an Eastern perspective, the mind can be seen as **consciousness**. Not to be handled, but rather *allowed:* "Let it be, and it will let you BE."

Where then lies the connecting bridge? Many schools of therapy, and psychosynthesis specifically, suggest that a distance between observer and mind is important to cultivate. What is clear, is that the greater the space and ability of the individual being to observe the mind, the greater the ease of handling undesirable behavior patterns. This is the linking of East with West. Develop an *observer* first and then a *witness* to the mind, and the individual can have more space between the witness and the mind.

The following meditations are designed to do just that, notice a witnessing presence, which yields no resistance to the mind and its movement.

Contemplate: *1.   I am not this psychic mechanism.*
                   2.   Experience yourself free of all thoughts and ideas.

Practice: Sit for about fifteen minutes for this meditation. Let your eyes close again. I want you to watch the thoughts that come through your awareness. I would like you to contemplate, "I am not this psychic mechanism," the mechanism of the mind. Contemplate that for a moment: I am not this psychic mechanism. Very gently, put your attention on your breath and notice the inhalation and the exhalation. For the next few moments, I would like you to meditate on yourself as being free from all thoughts and ideas. Imagine yourself being free from all thought constructs and ideas. When you are ready, return to the room.

Contemplate: 1. *That all information (knowledge) is with out cause.*

2. *The possibility that "This information (knowledge) does not belong to me personally."*

I'm using the words "knowledge" and "information" interchangeably here so that either word will suggest anything you know about yourself or the world. This meditation is suggested because in the *Shiva Sutras* it says "knowledge is bondage." Westerners misunderstand the word "knowledge," using the Western concept that knowledge has value. Actually what is meant is that *information* that you have about yourself is limiting when you define yourself by beliefs, thoughts, etc. Nisargadatta Maharaj used to say, "Anything you know about yourself is separate from you and should be discarded as *not you.*"

Practice: Let your eyes close. As any information about yourself comes into your awareness, contemplate that this information is without cause. Contemplate any information as being without any cause. Next, contemplate that this information does not belong to me. Whenever you re ready, bring your awareness back to the room, notice where you're sitting, and let your eyes open.

One student told me, "It's sort of a sticky issue for me, because I think I've never felt that anything came from cause or that I see things connect the way most people see them. It has sometimes made me feel as if I were crazy. To think that the way we function is from cause and effect could be a grounding mechanism, but I've never had that to ground myself with. It's never meant anything to me. I'm scared that if nothing connects, then my whole perception of reality gets screwed, and then I feel really weird." I commented that, "It becomes different from everybody else's."

"Yes," she continued, "I don't know how anything is related to anything else. What's related to water? So, it would have been harder if you had said to contemplate the fact that information does have a cause.

She added, "Nothing connects in the way we think it does. Where I get stuck is that I can take it even farther and say that nothing seems to have meaning, but I don't buy that either because, on deeper level, it has a very deep meaning."

Another student reported, "My experience was that there was no power in my thoughts or ideas or knowledge, nothing connected to them." I replied, "My hunch is that if you take your power back from thoughts, like taking it back from people, you'll feel more powerful." That's true for me. In other words, if you have been in a relationship in which how you felt about yourself was dependent upon how the other person felt about you at that moment, they had the power. Your "okayness" was dependent upon them. In the same way, if you have a thought called, "I want to go to Hawaii on a vacation," and give your power to that, then that will have power over you. The next thing you know is you're working overtime to pay for your trip to Hawaii, and who has the power? The trip to Hawaii has the power, because you're compelled by it; but you can pull your energy from it, and then it will have no power over you and you can do it or not do it.

Another student said, "I like the idea that this information does not belong to me. But, the only question I have is, if it doesn't belong to me, then who does it belong to?" I said, "Notice how you imagine and assume that there has to be an owner. We will look at this more in depth with the meditation: There are thoughts."

One student said, "I couldn't help but translate, 'This thought has no cause' into 'This thought has no source.' Then I said that I generate not only thoughts but, as a scientist, I generate facts. To say that they don't have a source is to say that I don't exist. I couldn't deal with it." "The *'I'* can't deal with it, for sure," I said.

Contemplate: *Knowledge or information not only appears in me; all objects have knowledge or information.*
(*Vijnana Bhairava,* Jaideva Singh)

Practice: Feeling your body supported and noticing your breathing, I would like you now to contemplate for fifteen minutes whatever information you imagine you have about yourself. For example, you're a woman or you re a man, or you're tall or you're short, or fat or thin, or some other piece of functional information. Take a moment to contemplate that information. Now contemplate that not only do I have information about myself, but all objects, i.e., pictures, couches, chairs, lamps—everything has information inside itself about itself. Now letting your *eyes open,* I'd like you to look around the room imagining that everything—couches and chairs, everything, has information about itself. You might want to imagine what that information is.

Contemplate: *1 What is the mind?*
2. *Bondage is a thought construct or idea.*
   (Vijnana Bhairava, Jaideva Singh)
3. *Liberation is a thought construct or idea.*
   (Vijnana Bhairava, Jaideva Singh)

Practice: Sit comfortably and let your eyes close for about fifteen minutes, again feeling your body being supported physically and feeling your breath. For the next few minutes contemplate: What is the mind? Next, con-

template that bondage is a thought construct or an idea or a belief. Contemplate
bondage as a thought construct or a belief.
For a moment, contemplate that *liberation*
is a thought construct or a belief. Feeling
your back and your body pressed and supported and feeling your breath, let yourself become aware of the room. Whenever
you're ready to come up, let your eyes
begin to open.

Contemplate: *Since time is a concept, change the
word—to the word "existence.*
(Vijnana Bhairava, Jaideva Singh)

Practice: *As* you begin to use this method, I'd like
you to first look at your concepts of time
and then switch a word in the process and
see what you experience. First, look at
the concept of time, and all your beliefs
about time. You can start off with, "Time
is_____ " and fill in the blank. When
you have about half a dozen ideas, go back
over your concepts of time, but change
the word "time" to "existence." So, for
instance, see what "There isn't enough
time for me," does for your experience
and then change the word "time" to ''existence'' and notice what happens. When
you are ready, come back to the room.

Here are some comments I've received from students in my classes: "Well, I got a feeling that time is something that we invented to ground us." ... "I got *Time is short,* and when I changed it to existence, existence is timeless. I stayed on that for a long time." ... "I found that the concept of time started out in an intellectual place, and then I found that time is limiting, and I started feeling very angry at the whole concept of time. When I switched it to existence, I became angry when I filled in the blank with existence is limiting. The same anger came, and I couldn't get out of it; I felt as if my throat was swelling up, like elephantiasis or something—so much anger about limitations."

What is it that Ram Dass said? "Before you can get out of the jail, first you have to realize that you're in one." First, you have to realize you're in it before you can get out. When I brought this idea up, a student said, "But sometimes they say you've got to accept where you are before you can get out of it. If you're constantly rejecting where you are, that keeps you stuck there."

When I was in India, a woman said to me, "I'm rejecting this, I'm rejecting that, I'm rejecting this, I should be accepting it." I said, "Why don't you accept the fact that you're rejecting it?" She changed immediately, because she accepted her rejecting. To say, "I'm rejecting it, and that's wrong because I should be accepting it" is like beating yourself up twice instead of once.

Meteditate: *Every time a thought comes into your awareness, imagine yourself putting it into a jar.*
(Vijnana Bhairava, Jaideva Singh)

Practice: Let your eyes close and every time a thought or an emotion comes into your awareness, imagine yourself putting it into a jar. Imagine putting all of your thoughts, feelings, sensations into a jar. Continue to put all thoughts, anything that comes into your awareness, into a jar. Gently, bring your awareness back to the room, and let your eyes open.

Meditate: *Every time a thought comes through your awareness, imagine it becoming the sky.*
(Vijnana Bhairava, Jaideva Singh)

Practice: Feeling your body supported and noticing your breathing, move into a quiet space. Now watch the thoughts that come through your awareness and every time a thought comes through your awareness, imagine it becoming the sky~ Every time a thought comes through your awareness, no matter what it is, imagine it becoming the sky. Gently, become aware of where your body is, and your breath, and, when-

ever you're ready, bring your awareness
back to the room, and let your eyes gently
open.

DESIRES

8 / DESIRES

Desire: To long for; to wish for earnestly; to covet; to hope for, as to desire riches, a friend, another's land, etc.

Desires, from my point of view, can be described in several ways. First, a desire can occur at a point in a child's development. For example, notice an infant or a young child. Most of their wanting is to relieve biological pain, like hunger or cold. Or a need to fill a lack, like wanting a hug to feel safe. Later in life, the child uses what is called transitional objects like blankets, teddies, pillows, which they carry around as "substitute friends" so they don't have to feel separate or alone.

Another perspective equates desire with resistance. Stated another way, if you desire something it is a resisted experience. For example, a child that is always labeled as bad, no good, etc., might *overcompensate* and develop a desire for fame and money to prove "I am good." However, the desire is never fully quenched since it is trying to handle "I am bad," which is the unwanted experience, by resisting it, by believing money is good. Therefore, "I'm good if I have it" is then used to overcompensate for the resisted experience. This gives Buddha's Noble Truth *"Be Desireless,"* a new meaning—instead of *Be Desireless: Don't Resist.*

The above utilizes psychological explanations, but for the practitioner of Inner Transmutation, desires are merely energy or **consciousness** in a different shape or form. From this perspective, with no label, desires, wishes or wants are just what they are—namely, energy or **consciousness**. As the practice begins to deepen, spiritual aspirants develop a non-judgmental approach of exploring their desires, as opposed to trying to get rid of them, overcome them, deny them, transform them. Instead, to see them as made of "energy" or **consciousness**. Many desires are to relieve biological and emotional pain. Problems arise later in life when we try to *substitute* one pain reliever for another. For example, when we feel a lack of love, rather than experiencing the loneliness, we eat or have sex. Often, status symbols like big houses or cars are pain relievers for feeling a lack of self-worth. This is how desires escalate and get distorted.

Meditate: *Focus your attention on the energy of desire rather than on the object of the desire.*

Now we're going to work with desires. I know you don't have any, but imagine that you do!

A student asked, "I want to be free of things that hold me back. Is that a desire?" I suggested that he use that for this meditation. Use whatever desire you have. It could be "I want to be free," whatever it is. It could be your desire for a pizza, it could be a desire for something to happen in your life.

Practice: Let your eyes close. We're going to run two meditations because I like the way they fit. Allow an object of extreme desire to come into your mind. Imagine it is out in front of you. It could be a person, it could be a situation, anything that you want. Notice what the object or situation or experience looks like and sounds like. Feel or notice sensations or feelings, the sensations inside your body associated with that particular desire. Now, very gently, I'd like you to focus your attention on the energy called desire itself, noticing its size or shape, rather than the fantasized desire in your mind. Focus your awareness on the desire inside you, the energy or sensations called "desire" inside, rather than on the desired object. Pull your attention inside to the desire itself and watch the desire *as energy* inside you. Meditate on the desire as energy. Continue to focus your attention on the desire as energy, and watch the energy called "desire."

A student asked if he should see desire as something negative. I replied that desire is desire. There is no bad or good about it, it's just energy.

I would suggest that as you go through your life in the next few days, you work with any desire coming into your awareness. Suppose you are driving your car and you notice a new Porsche. All of a sudden, for that moment, your desire is called "I want a Porsche," or you might see that Porsche in your mind's eye. Some people, when they focus on the Porsche, will do every-thing possible in the universe to make that desire come true. It could be a relationship. It could be new clothes, it could be a job, it could be any one of a thousand particular things. Rather than focusing on the Porsche, I would like for you to pull your attention from the desired object—the Porsche or the new job or the rela-tionship and turn it toward the energy itself inside your body. When there is a sense of "I want a Porsche" or "I want a relationship," or whatever, meditate on the energy itself inside your body.

If you continue to meditate on, say, the relationship, you're always out there looking for a relationship. If you focus your attention on the energy itself, my expe-rience has been that you can either have the relation-ship or not have the relationship, and that either way it's okay. That's what I mean by focusing on the energy of the desire, rather that on the desired object. Most people have a desire—it doesn't matter what it is—and they'll spend most of their lives reacting to that desire and spend all of their time trying to fulfill it externally.

If you turn your attention inside and focus on the energy of desire, the energy transmutes. Then you can either *have it* or *not have it,* and it won't really matter much to you. Your internal state will remain the same.

Meditate: Step 1: Notice a desire for something (car, lover, etc.)

Step 2: Feel the desire for that object.

Step 3: Experience the desire as made of energy or **consciousness**.

Step 4: Notice that you are the observer.

Step 5: Experience the object of desire as made of the same **consciousness** as the energy of desire.

Step 6: Experience the desire and the observer as made of the same **consciousness** as the energy of desire and the desired object.

Meditate: 1. Experience your body as empty space.

2. Pull your attention from any thought by not allowing it to settle. It disappears.
(Vijnana Bhairava, Jaideva Singh)

Practice: Let your eyes close. Imagine your body is empty space. *As* you're noting that your body is empty space, become aware of whatever thoughts, either pleasant or unpleasant, that come through your awareness. Whatever thought comes through your awareness, gently pull your attention back from it. Pull your attention—away from any thought, and do not allow it to settle down inside yourself. Notice how it disappears.

When the thought is not allowed to settle down, it loses support and dissolves. So every time a thought comes through your awareness, gently take your attention off of it; when you don't allow it to settle, it begins to lose support and dissolve. Whatever thought comes through your awareness, wherever the mind goes, gently pull your attention from that thought. Whenever you re ready, let your eyes open.

A student commented after this meditation, "I'm aware that my body's relaxed and tired." Another student told me, "I felt so serene and open. And I found that I had few thoughts, like birds flying by."

Contemplate: *Desires do not only appear inside me; they also appear inside other objects.*

This last one is one of my favorite open-eyed meditations. The meditations starts off with 10 minutes with eyes closed and then finishes with 10 minutes with eyes open.

Practice: Feeling your body being physically supported, watch your breath. Witness and notice a parade of your desires. Watch them from a distance, as if you were in a movie theater watching them on the screen. Again, watch from a great distance. Take a few minutes to do that. Contemplate that desires don't only appear inside of you, but that all objects—chairs, couches, pictures, lamps, everything—has desires. For a moment, imagine everything as having desires. Very gently, let your eyes open. And imagine all the objects in the room to have desires. Imagine what those desires are. Continue to look at the different objects and imagine what their deepest desire is. See if you can keep that awareness for a few minutes.

"When I did this meditation, I eventually got to a chair wanting to be a chair and a couch wanting to be a couch. I always imagine that a couch wants to be a chair, and the chair wants to be a different color!"

A student comment: "I got the basic impression that everything desired to be. It was very freeing to realize that, because it was as if everybody and everything wants to exist. Then I asked myself, Why are we always doing this stuff about things not existing, and that whole side of Indian, or whatever, philosophy? I decided it was better to concentrate on the being, or the 'is-ness', or whatever. And that was very nice; it was as if going beyond our initial desire to exist gets too complicated."

I replied, "It's very difficult to be in the world and practice Vedanta. It's much easier to practice Kashmir Shaivism or Tantric Yoga. That is why some yogis have a hard time implanting themselves in America. It's very difficult to say to Americans or Western Europeans or Australians, 'not this, not this.' It is difficult to say to a Westerner who is paying his rent and having relationships; "this is *not real"…"It's all a mirage."*

This is a very important point in understanding the context in which a spiritual path develops. Most people in India who practice yoga follow the *neti, neti,* or not this, not this approach. Why? Because in India, the weather is terrible, health is terrible, and poverty is overwhelming. In fact, CNN news recently reported that the life expectancy in India is age 37. Naturally then, their spiritual philosophy would be, *not this, please not this.*

A small percentage of yoga practitioners live in Kashmir. There, the food is good, health is good, weather is good, and it is probably one of the most beautiful places in the world. In Kashmir the yoga practice is Kashmir Shaivism or Tantric yoga. Their philosophy is one of inclusion or *"and this, and this."* Notice how the context shapes the spiritual path rather than the other way around. And that the spiritual path becomes a justification for psychological survival, given the context. In other words, to justify life in the horrible poverty of India *"not this"* is a spiritual survival mechanism explained by the context.

These are the types of questions that need to be explored by seekers as they attempt to bring an Eastern spiritual path into Western civilization, i.e., the context is greater than the individual and spiritual path. In other words, the spiritual path is created out of the context the individual lives in. For this reason, each person at some point must tailor-make their own spiritual path, rather than trying to take on an *entire* spiritual path which came out of a different cultural context. Guidance, however, is important, otherwise it is easy for "one" to unknowingly re-enforce their unconscious structure.

DEATH

9 / DEATH

In many traditions, particularly that of Tibetan Buddhism, death *is* an important component. In the *Tibetan Book of the Dead,* the *bardo* is the name for the in-between state, the state between death and life, is discussed at length. There are also several other bardos (in-between states) which bear mention. The space between two thoughts, the space between two breaths, the space between waking and dreaming, the space between dreaming and deep sleep, the space between deep sleep and waking, and the space between life and death. In Tibetan Buddhism, the space between death and life is emphasized. To emphasize further, a course of action is recommended for attaining liberation in the after-death state. Needless to say, in Western cultures, death has become the unmentionable and the most *denied* experience of life.

From "my" perspective, the most dissociated or disowned part of existence is death. Most religions offer their model or metaphor of the after-life; all are laden with fear and superstition. If an individual could process or release these belief structures and know that death is part of existence, life could be experienced more fully, and existence could be experienced as a *WHOLE*. In the course of my own search years ago, I went to Nepal to learn the preparation for death and death (bardo) practices. For several years I worked in this way, and it transformed my experience of life. Why? Because the present-time experience of life becomes much more whole, intense and real when death is included as a part of life, rather than something to be feared and denied.

Meditate: *Imagine that the world is coming to an end and that there are only ten minutes left to live.*

This meditation is a first one for starting the work on death. The purpose of these meditations is to begin to get in touch with your belief system about what death is going to be like, and to notice that they are only beliefs, ideas, thoughts, thought constructs to be witnessed, and then to notice what happens as you do the meditation.

Practice: Meditate for ten minutes. Begin by feeling your body being physically supported. Continue to notice your breath. Now imagine yourself walking down a country road and heading for home, and that you re not very far away from it. As you begin to get closer to home, you get closer to the outskirts of the city. Rather than seeing it on a movie screen with the small you walking, step into the person that's walking, so there's no small you on a screen but simply *you walking.* You might be able to notice the scenery as you're walking closer to home. Notice any sounds, as well as what it feels like to be heading in the direction of your home.

Suddenly a siren sounds, a very loud *air-raid siren,* and something inside you says that in a very short time, there is going to be a nuclear attack. You're able to head to the nearest air-raid shelter, which isn't too far from where you are. The siren is loud. Somehow, you find yourself inside the air-raid shelter and notice what it looks like. Notice the people in the shelter, if there are any, or maybe you're alone. You notice that there is only enough air for about ten minutes, and that you therefore have only have ten minutes to live. Notice what your experience is during your last ten minutes. (Give yourself about thirty seconds between each minute.) You only have nine minutes left to live. You only have eight minutes left. Seven minutes left to live. Six minutes to live. Five minutes left. Four minutes left. Three minutes left. Two minutes left. One minute left to live.

> That's it—you're dead. Very gently, when-
> ever you're ready, bring your awareness
> back to the room and let your eyes gently
> open.

One student commented after this meditation that she hadn't wanted to suffocate in the fallout shelter, "so I went back outside and figured that when the bomb dropped, I'd go. But the time was nice. It felt like antici-pation. The whole feeling was nice, and the feeling in my body, but when you said, 'That's it,' it was like noth-ing. I couldn't imagine 'That's it.'"

Another student reported, "I feel very fearful when-ever I hear sirens. I went into the bomb shelter with all of the people and wondered what was I doing in there. I got real quiet and everybody else disappeared. All of the noise disappeared. I was wondering what I was doing in there without my kids, though. I've had visions or dreams, you know, daydreams, sleeping dreams, things that come into my **consciousness**.

"One that I have had a few times is standing out on my back patio and looking up and suddenly notic-ing the funny light that's going on. I realize that they have dropped the bomb and in a split second, I go to my daughter, realizing what's happening, and that she's there, too, and that there's not even time to say what's going on or explain or anything. It's that fast. It's so real when you're looking into your kid's eyes."

Another student commented, "It's interesting that you have a sudden impact by saying, eight minutes. I was thinking of roses, a woman, and then when you said, 'Eight minutes,' my hands got clammy, and everything else. Then I started thinking of sharks eating me in the water, and like that. Then when you said we were dead, I felt as if I was floating through space. It was very peaceful and a feeling of lightness came.

Another student said, "I experienced a whole series of things. At ten, I was almost banging on the walls, and then, around nine, I got really sad. Somewhere around seven, I felt grief, and then there was a sense of 'I'm all right now.' However, this was not acceptance, but all of this defiance, and I was ready for it. Then, when I was dead, I was angry. I didn't realize how angry I was. It was like all of these vignettes of past lives, and I realized there is still a lot of blame in me toward mankind and the kind of bullshit that goes on—the wars and the stupidities. I was really angry. I didn't leave with a feeling of 'Oh, I'm at peace.' It wasn't complete, either. I didn't feel completion. I felt really annoyed."

Another student: "During the first part of the countdown, I was not focusing as I should have but then there was such a space between numbers, there was nothing else to do, so I got into it and started looking at my life. I realized I've had a real good time, but I don't think I was dealing with death yet, so when you said, 'You're dead,' I had a sudden physical reaction as if I was going to leave my body. Then inside something said, No, I'm not. Then a reply from inside:

Oh yes, you are. I felt a physical pull, and I was staying grounded. I swallowed, and that helped me be grounded. Then I wondered if maybe that does happen sometimes—that when someone dies they have a hard time leaving their body or whether it's an automatic thing."

A student commented, "I really enjoyed this meditation because I felt so sad at the beginning that we were all gasping for breath and how much I loved them and all of the things I hadn't said and done, and blah, blah, blah. Then, at the very end, it was the greatest freeing feeling, coming out of the body and leaving the pain of the sobbing." Recently, I was watching TV and wondered what I would do if the news of nuclear attack came over the Emergency Broadcasting System. My immediate thought was that I would sit down and meditate and that it was the way I would personally want it to be if there were only fifteen or twenty minutes left.

Meditate: *On a red spark from the cremation fire leaping up into your third eye.*

Practice: This is one of the more powerful meditations. Get yourself comfortable and sit for a while. Very gently, let your eyes close and feel your body, how it is situated, and notice the rising and falling of your breath. Now imagine yourself, around eveningtime, walking down a country road; you might even be able to hear the sound of your own footsteps. Rather than watch a small you on a screen, walking down a country road, step inside the skin of that person, so that you're actually *doing it*. As you are walking, you can see the gates of a graveyard in the distance. You can see the tombstones. In the far distance is a cremation fire, and on either side are bodies either waiting to be burned or partially burned. You walk toward the cremation fire and stand in front of it. Make sure you're behind your own eyes, actually standing there, rather than seeing a small you standing there. Notice the temperature change in front of the fire, and the smell. You may be even hearing the crackling of the fire, looking directly into it, smelling all of the smells of the fire. The fire gets a little lighter since there are several bodies that are beginning to really burn up quite a bit.

Suddenly, a spark jumps from the fire and it lands on your third eye and begins to burn deeply, burning into your third eye. For the next few minutes, notice the temperature change in your third eye as it burns, and as the red light burns, notice how it feels, and how it looks as the red light lights up in your third eye.

Feeling your body pressed against the chair, and noticing your breathing, very gently, whenever you're ready, let yourself come back, and let your eyes begin to open.

Meditate: *Imagine that you're in a graveyard. Make it your home for the night.*

Practice: Continuing with our work on death, take a deep breath. Imagine that you're walking down a country road. In the distance are very large gates. You're walking toward a cemetery. As you walk, you notice that it's getting to be evening. You walk gently into the cemetery. It begins to get darker and darker, so that nightfall is really upon you. You decide to sleep there for the night. Find a place to sleep in the cemetery. Make a home in the cemetery for the night. Take your time as you make your home; notice if there are any energies that you can sense, see, or hear, as you begin to prepare yourself to lie down, or when you already are lying down to sleep. Now, being your own time, let the nighttime move toward morning. And whenever you feel finished, allow your eyes to open.

One student said, "That was a good one! I found a little place under a tree that was really nice, and the energies that I felt sort of became the zombies' forces. I experienced spring, and there were tulips and daffodils everywhere. Then there was summer and everything was green, and then there was fall, and then there was winter and there was snow; and when you said I had to come out of there, I didn't want to."

Another student commented, "I found that my fear of external things was so great that it was hard for me to see anything else. Finally, I had to create my dog being there with me. Then it was beautiful, and I went to the family plot, a nice little cozy corner to lie in. It was really comfortable, but I feared all of these people walking through; I felt comfortable with the dead people, but not with the other ones.

Another student reported, "At first I thought you were going to ask me if I saw my own grave, and for some reason I did see my own name on a tombstone. I thought it was funny that here I am quite alive and that the Emily body was dead." I asked whether the stone had a date on it. She continued, "No, I didn't look. The thing that was distressing was that I kept hearing voices, as if a lot of people were there, all of the many lifetimes they had lived, and voices and voices and voices. It was overwhelming, and I wished they would all shut up. There were so many lifetimes and so many people, like vibrations and the sound of voices or whispering that it was too much to deal with." I asked her if she ever experienced whispering voices. She said that she did, and I suggested that, at some point when she felt that same space, she could imagine the voices on a record and then practice speeding them up and slowing them down and notice what happened, if anything.

Another student had a similar experience: "I was feeling really good until an outside voice came in. It was my mother's voice, and she said that there are all of these things to be afraid of. Then I got this panicky feeling about the darkness and securing my own territory. I went through that whole trip of what could I do to make myself feel secure. I realized it was my mother's voice: it was very clear. It was really interesting."

I gave her the same practice. I told her that the voice was probably going on all the time outside of her awareness and said, "Suppose you're at home tomorrow and you're watching television, and you hear this voice, and whatever it says to you. See if you can speed it up and slow it down, to get a sense of playing with it. You can speed up the voice and slow it down, and see what your experience is when you do that."

One student got concerned that she might feel more comfortable with the dead than with the living. I suggested that, rather than put a meaning on what the internal voice said, she use the meditations in the early part of this book. I suggested that, when a thought came by that said "I feel more comfortable with the dead than with the living," rather than identifying with it, she could ask, "Who is this 'I' who is saying to itself, 'I feel more comfortable with the dead than with the living?'"

Meditate: *Throw yourself onto a cremation fire.*

Practice: Begin by noticing your back and body pressed and supported. Noticing the rising and falling of your breath, allow yourself to become more relaxed. I'd like you to imagine, to see, or to feel yourself walking down a country road toward a cemetery that is in the distance. As you walk toward the cemetery, you can hear your own footsteps, and you can hear the sound of your breathing. Night is falling. You enter the cemetery. noticing the grave stones. In the distance, you can see a cremation fire, and you begin to walk toward it. There are bodies that are already burned, and there are bodies stacked, waiting to be burned. You walk toward the funeral fire and stand directly in front of it, noticing its color. You will feel the temperature change, you could be hearing the sound, the crackling sound of the fire. You stand in front of the fire, gazing.

First, witness from a distance a little you who is standing in front of the funeral fire, so that you can watch the fire from a distance. Now, I'd like you to step into the skin of the person standing in front of the funeral fire, so that you can see from behind your eyes, clearly see the fire. Gently, whenever you're ready, allow yourself to throw yourself onto the fire. Experience what happens as your body burns and witness your body burning.

> Continue to witness your body burning; you might notice it being reduced to ashes, and the wind coming and blowing the ashes away. Gently, notice where you are sitting. Whenever you're ready, let your eyes gently open and come back to the room.

A student commented that when I said to look at the flames, she was already in the fire. "Even before you said that, my body was in it; and it was a sense of melting. Maybe that's not it, but it was really easy." I asked, "After the body melted, were you there watching?" She answered, "Just watching."

"I enjoyed that," she continued. "It felt really liberating. There was a moment there where I watched some of my old skin disappear, and it was as if I shriveled up, but it didn't have anything to do with me. It was fun to watch myself watching it. Then you said to jump in. First, I couldn't imagine what it would feel like to burn, physically, so I didn't feel it physically. When I was watching, I had trouble seeing the body dissolve, because I don't think I've ever seen a body do that. But I love fire. All of a sudden, we had to have it gone, so pretty rapidly it was just ashes."

I asked, "Did you experience yourself watching at that point? There was nothing there in that space? Or you watching? In other words, after the body was gone, was it your experience of watching?" She said yes, but that she realized she still had the illusion of having some kind of body, even if it wasn't physical. "I thought I should see another dimension or there better be something else to this."

Another comment: "I noticed that the body was not really hot but that whatever it was that was watching me wasn't identifying with the heat." I replied, "The *Bhagavad Gita,* referring to the self, says, 'Swords can't cut it and fire can't burn it.'"

CONTEMPLATION

10 / CONTEMPLATION

Contemplation: "A state of awareness of God's being or presence. An act of mind in considering with attention, continued attention to a particular subject, meditation." (Webster's *American College Dictionaiy*).

In this section, it is through deep contemplation that an individual is able to experience the being-ness, or inner witness, which is behind all actions. It is a paradox to be able to utilize the focus of one s mind to cultivate that which is behind actions, words, thoughts, and feelings. For example, as a child, one might have experienced utilizing a magnifying glass to focus the sun's rays in order to burn a leaf. In the same way, through *focus of attention* in a specific way, with intention, the mind can burn through ideas and beliefs so that you can go beyond the mind.

Meditate: *On yourself as free from thought constructs.*

(Vijnana Bhairava, Jaideva Singh)

Practice: Feel your body being supported, and notice your breathing, the rising and falling of your breath. Focus your attention on yourself as free from all thought constructs. Meditate on yourself as free from all thought constructs, and you can be free of ideas about yourself. Very gently, begin to bring your awareness back to the room, and begin to let your eyes open.

A student commented, "I saw the thought constructs as hooks in my mind; some seemed harder to release than others, and I realized they were more like fishhooks, like little barbs. It was pretty interesting." Another student said, "I had a hard time when you said to be free of all thought constructs. It was as if, as soon as I was given permission to be free, I went through *all these tapes about why I couldn't be free.* I couldn't imagine being free." I told this student to notice the beliefs such as "I can't be free" and experience them as energy, or ask, "Whose thoughts are these?" or "Who told you that?"—THE MIND.

I was once sitting with Baba Prakashananda in Bombay. He and I were the only ones in the room. All of a sudden, he started to focus his attention on me, which felt like energy was pouring into me. It felt like I was on fire. He was looking at me, and my body started to burn up. I was in incredible psychic agony, psychic pain, and I really held onto the rug. I had decided that he was doing something, I didn't know what it was. He got more and more intense, and I thought I was going to go crazy. He was looking down at me, which of course made it even worse. I waited for something, some belief structure, to emerge from beneath my usual awareness. What came by was, "I'm sorry that I am." I looked at it, witnessed it, watched it arise and subside, and it disappeared. I felt finished and in a completely different state. I touched his feet and left about a minute later. What was true was that I had walked around my whole life unknowingly saying to myself, "I'm sorry that I am." That had been my unconscious mantra, and I had walked around experiencing that. There are two reasons I tell this story. First, I tell it to point out the process of things emerging from underneath our usual awareness—from that ninety percent of our minds that are "under water" like an iceberg, an analogy I referred to earlier in this book. Second, when I started meditating in groups, I noticed that the issues and patterns were pushed up more because the energy is a little bit stronger in groups than when meditating alone. Although ultimately you must do it alone, at the beginning it can be done in groups.

I have noticed, being around certain teachers, they pushed me in a certain way that forced me to look at my belief structures that I might not have ordinarily questioned.

One time when I was in India, I was sitting with Baba Prakashananda and he started playing with me. He was sitting there and trying to *hook me*. A friend said she felt like she was beaten up psychically, but I

felt as if he was playing with me, to try to *hook me*
Whatever he did, I noticed what belief came up and
internally I'd ask, "Who is this I?" No matter what he
threw at me. After two or three minutes, he left me
alone and started with other people.

The purpose of all these methods is to be able to
unhook. Begin to discard your old belief structures so
that you can witness more, and be free.

Meditate: *Create a dream fantasy of yourself and an*
enlightened being.

For this meditation, I am going to use the term
"realized being" and "enlightened being" interchangeably. I want you to think of someone that you have met
or can imagine, living or dead, a woman or man, who
might be in that state of awareness, a state of enlighten-
ment. It could be Jesus or Buddha or anyone.

Practice: Once again, feel your body, how it is
seated, and notice the rising and falling
of your breath. For the next few minutes,
I want you to create a dream fantasy of
yourself and an enlightened being, a realized being. You can be doing anything.
You could be taking a walk; you could be
going on a hike or swimming or driving in
your car or going to the movies. For the
next few minutes, create a dream fantasy
of yourself and a realized being together,

doing whatever it is you would like to do. You might hear or feel the energy, but notice the internal shift as you imagine yourself and a realized being spending some time together. Notice the energy, the feeling or the sound or what the energy looks like. Continue to allow yourself to have this dream fantasy of you and a realized being, feeling, hearing or seeing the energy. Now, I'd like you to take the hand of that enlightened being, and, holding that hand, I would like you to pull that realized being toward you and merge with her or him so that you and the realized being are one, and you can experience that person's body and your physical body being the same body.

Meditate: *On religious symbols.*
Find the space or void before the emergence of any religious symbols.

The purpose of this meditation is to process out either negative or positive reactions you have to particular religious or spiritual symbols, such as crosses, Jewish stars, mandalas, statues, crystals. I am going to ask you to find a religious symbol inside yourself. It doesn't matter what it is. You'll be surprised how much attachment you have, with either good or bad feelings (energy) attached to it. I want you then to go back into the space from which the symbol arose, to the space prior to the symbol and meditate on that space or void.

Practice: Take a deep breath. Then I'd like you to create an image, or let an image come to you, of a spiritual or religious symbol. Notice what your positive or negative feelings are about it. Then find the void prior to the emergence of that symbol. Then let another religious symbol come up into your awareness; notice the image, good or bad, and find the space that symbol came from. Now let another religious symbol come up into your awareness, notice the energy, and find the space that symbol came from. Allow another spiritual symbol to come into your awareness, and again, locate the space that symbol came from. And finally, one more religious symbol: notice the energy attached to it, and find the space and stay in the space where all religious symbols come from; in fact, stay in the space where all symbols come from. Go deeply into that space. Go deeply into the void prior to the emergence of any or all symbols. Whenever you're ready, begin coming up and back, bringing your awareness back to the room, and allow your eyes to open.

A student commented, "That was really refreshing. It was kind of like going into outer space. I saw all of these symbols spilling around, and I would create a feeling about one and throw it back, and there was always that space." I recall what the comedian George Carlin said about symbols: "Symbols are for the symbol-minded."

Meditate: *Find the space between two breaths.*

In this meditation, you watch your breath. It's a very simple meditation. I want you to watch your breath rise. You will inhale, there will be a space before the inhale turns to an exhale, and you will exhale and there will be a space before your exhale turns into an inhale: Inhale, space, exhale, space; Inhale, space, exhale, space. It will be the same space each time.

The important part of the meditation is to focus your attention on the space between two breaths.

In 1977 Swami Muktananda taught us "So-ham" mantra. At the time he said you repeat to yourself "So" on the inhale and "Ham" on the exhale. *Soham* means I *AM* THAL Several years later, Swami Muktananda, in a book, suggested the reverse, the "Ham-sa" mantra, i.e., inhale on "Ham" and exhale on "So". *Hamsa* means THAT I AM.

In the late 70's I got involved more with the feminine and discovered "Sa-ham" mantra, which means I AM SHE. All of these meditations are widely used in India, but again, what is ultimately most important is to focus your attention on the space between two breaths. This is the changeless underlying unity which leads to what I later called Quantum Consciousness.

I once asked Nisargadatta Maharaj about the mantra "So-ham." He said, "It means 'I Am That,' which is a concept." I said I didn't understand. He said, "If I write down on a piece of paper, 'ten pounds of gold,' is that the same as gold? You must meditate past your concepts!"

So the experience of the space between two breaths is what is important, or the space before or after the repetition of the mantra—not *the mantra itself.*

Meditate: *1. I-I-I*
2. Me-Me-Me
3. Mine-Mine-Mine

For the first one, I'd like you to repeat, over and over again like a mantra: "I, 1,1, I." The mantra is going to be that followed by the other two listed above.

Practice: So again, allow your eyes to close and notice how you're sitting. And then go back to your breath for a second; notice the rising and falling. Now, begin to repeat, "I, I, I, I," over and over again. And as you continue to repeat "I, I, I," you will be able to witness the "I." Continue to repeat, "I, I, I, I." And now change it to "me, me, me, me," and witness the constant repetition of the "me, me, me." And now, repeat "mine, mine, mine, mine, mine, mine, mine, mine." And very gently, bring your awareness back to the room. Whenever you're ready, open your eyes.

One student said, "It didn't have much energy, except that it set off a vibration that went through my body every time I said it. But, when I got to *me,* I felt like a kid; there was something wanting to go 'Whee!' And with 'mine,' I was on the verge of hysteria, like 'MINE!' I don't know what it was, but it was like, 'Don't touch it, don't try to take it.'"

I asked this student if she was able to watch it. She answered, "Yes, I was watching it, but I don't know what it was exactly. Both of the last two put me in the frame of a three-year-old. It was interesting because there was a lot of energy behind it."

There is a wonderful article, called "The Secret of Renunciation," in Swami Muktananda's book *Play of Consciousness.* In that book Muktananda says you don't have to renounce your job or your family or your relationships: renounce your identification with the "I, the me, and the mine." By "renouncing," he meant to let go of your identification attachment to "I, me, mine."

Meditate: *1.* There are *thoughts, rather then* my *thoughts.*
   2. There are *feelings, rather than* my *feelings.*
   3. There is *life, rather than* my *life.*

1. Being thought rather than thinking.
2. Being felt rather than feeling.
3. Being lived rather than living.

Practice: There are several different phases of this meditation, so sit for about 30 minutes, spending three to five minutes on each part. Let your eyes close, and feel your body being supported by either the seat or the floor, watching the rising and falling of your breath. As you begin to notice thoughts go through your awareness, begin to say to yourself, "There are thoughts." Rather than being identified with the content of them, as thoughts go through your awareness, gently say, "There are thoughts." Continue to contemplate as you say to yourself, "There are thoughts." If feelings begin to happen, gently say, "There are feelings," seeing them in the distance. If thoughts of life come up, or if anything comes up, begin to say to yourself, "There is life." Rather than "My life," say "There is life."

Nisargadatta said to me, "The problem is that you identify yourself as a person in life, rather than witnessing that there is life, which actually has nothing to do with you, so you should stay out of it." Now, bring your attention back to your breath.

I'd like you to contemplate *being thought,* rather than "I am thinking." Contemplate *being thought,* rather than "I am thinking," and, rather than "I am feeling," contemplate *being felt.* Now, rather than "I am feeling," contemplate *being felt;* and, rather than "I am living," contemplate *being lived.*

Feeling your body pressed against the floor or the couch or the chair, and noticing your breath, bring your attention very gently back to the room and, whenever you're ready, let your eyes gently open.

Meditate:
1. *On the void above you.*
2. On the void below you.
3. On the void to the right of you.
4. On the void to the left of you.
5. On the void ahead of you.
6. *On the void behind you.*

Practice: Feel your body again being supported, and notice your breath rising and falling. I'd like you to meditate on the void above you, as though outer space were directly above you, say from your shoulders up. Focus your attention on the void above you. Now, focus your attention on the void below you. Focus your attention on the void below you. Now, focus your attention on the void to the right of you. Focus your attention on the void to your right. Now, I'd like you to focus your attention on the void to the left. Now, focus your attention on the void in front of you, almost as though you're looking into the void: and focus all of your attention on the void in front of you, completely in front of you. Almost as if you're sitting on the edge, looking into the void. Continue to focus on the void in front of you.

In one gesture, let the void be simultaneously in front of you, behind you, above you and below you, in all directions; inside of you and outside of you, in all directions. Let everything be void all at once, simultaneously in all directions, everything void. Continue to focus your attention on the void extending in every direction, all at once, simultaneously. Now, experience the void inside your body. Now, experiencing the void inside your body, the void in all directions, allow your skin boundary to become the void.

Finally, now experience the knower of all this as void. Notice your breath, letting it come up to your chest a little bit, and then feel your body being physically supported by the couch or the seat or by the floor. And, very gently, whenever you're ready, let your eyes begin to open.

Meditate: *1. On the void at the end of the mantra.*
2. On the third eye, breathing into the crown of the head by building a bridge.

                    (Vijnana Bhairava, Jaideva Singh)

In this meditation we are going to repeat a mantra, but rather than focusing your attention on it, I want you to focus on the space after the mantra. Use any mantra you like; you can use "Om," if you like. Say the mantra to yourself, and then focus your attention on the space after it. Find the void after the mantra. Sit for about 30 minutes.

Practice: So, first feel your body, how it is sitting, and focus your attention on your breath. Begin to repeat the mantra. I would like you for a few minutes to place your attention on the void after the mantra.

        Now I'd like you to imagine that your third eye has nostrils on it, like a nose, so that you can inhale and exhale through the nostrils in your third eye. Imagine yourself breathing in and out through the nostrils that are in your third eye. Continue to imagine yourself inhaling and exhaling through the nostrils in your third eye.

And now, as you inhale through the third eye, imagine there is a bridge being built from your third eye to the crown of your head. Now when you inhale through the third eye, your breath goes up the bridge to the crown of your head. When you exhale, it goes down the bridge from the crown to the third eye and out the third eye. And you can regulate your breath going from the third eye up the bridge, then down the bridge and out your third eye. You can continue to inhale through the third eye, the breath going up the bridge to the crown and down the bridge and out the third eye, as that happens with the regularity of your breath rising and falling. In your own time, gently come back to the room and let your eyes open.

Meditate: *Imagine the elements (earth, water; fire, air, ether) being sucked up into the void at the crown of your head.*

From the Indian point of view, there are five elements: earth, water, air, fire, ether.

Practice: We start off again by how you feel, where your body is physically; your feet, where they are physically. Begin to notice your breath. What you can do first is to experience the void at the crown of your head. Focus your attention on the crown of your head as a void, totally void. Focus your attention on the void in the crown of your head.

Now, imagine all of the earth element in your body gradually being sucked up into the void at the crown of your head. Allow the earth element to be sucked into the void at the crown of your head, until all of the earth element has been sucked into the void at the crown of your head.

Now, imagine all of the water element in your body being drawn up into the void at the crown of your head. Let all the water element be drawn up into the void at the crown of your head. Now, allow all of the fire element, all the fire, to be drawn up into the void at the crown of your head.

Now, imagine all the air element being drawn up into the void at the crown of your head. All the air element being drawn into the void at the crown of your head.

The ether—allow it to be drawn into the void at the crown of your head. And any thoughts, let them be drawn up into the void at the crown of your head. Any feelings, sensations that might be left, allow them to be drawn up into the void at the crown of your head. And finally, let your entire awareness move into the void at the crown of your head. Continue to allow your awareness to go up and out into the void at the crown of your head.

Gently, feeling your body being supported, feeling your breath, bring your awareness back to the room and let your eyes open.

A student commented, "I found that when the earth was removed in the beginning, I could feel it moving up from my fingers; I could actually feel it going through my body. With the fire and water, I started feeling teary. Then when the air started getting pulled out, it was all I could do not to vomit. My whole body wanted to vomit." I asked her if the nausea could move out through the top of the head. She answered, "Possibly. I found that there didn't seem to be much left down here. It was as if all there was left was the nausea." Another option for her is to focus attention on the nausea, to watch it as energy **consciousness** in a different shape or form. It's important to remember that when doing any form of meditation you can use the self-enquiry or transmutation approach, i.e., seeing *anything* as made of energy or **consciousness** in a different shape or form to assist you through any "stuck" places. Meditate on the nausea as energy. I got really sick one night—I'd eaten yogurt malt balls! I don't know how many I ate, but I wrote my will out in about five minutes. I didn't

know whether I was going to have vomiting or diar-
rhea—it was that intense. I pulled all my attention,
really intensely with everything I had, into the space
before I felt sick. I then felt the nausea as energy. It was
about two minutes before the energy shifted and I didn't
feel sick anymore. My suggestion is to put your attention on the nausea rather than on whatever movie you're
running in your mind about the nausea. Turn your attention toward the nausea itself and watch it as energy in a
contracted form, without the intention of getting rid of
it. View it as energy and see what happens.

In response, a student said, "I'll try." I said, "That's
what I'm afraid of!"

Meditate: 1. *Imagine your physical body as empty
space.*
(Vijnana Bhairava, Jaideva Singh)

2. *Contemplate the non-essentiality of the
universe.*
(Vijnana Bhairava, Jaideva Singh)

Practice: Meditate and focus your attention on your
physical body and meditate on it as empty
space. Imagine your physical body as
empty space. Continue to imagine your
skin, your flesh, and your body and bones
as empty space. Keeping your eyes closed,
I would like you to contemplate the non-
essentiality of the universe. For the next

few minutes, contemplate the possibility that the universe is non-essential.

Gently, feet your body, where it is, noticing your breathing, and very gently, bring your awareness back to the room. And whenever you're ready, let your eyes open.

A student commented, "I was thinking that everything is a manifestation of something else, that it really is not essential. It was as if it was there, and I didn't have to do anything with or about it."

CONCLUSION

CONCLUSION

How can I conclude that which has no end? I remember the frustration, and then the freedom, when I realized "that anything conceived or understood can't be it." When Nisargadatta was asked, "Who are you?" he replied, "I am nothing perceivable or conceivable and anything you think I am, I am not." In the *Avadhuta Stotram* it says that the Avadhuta or someone immersed in that state of **consciousness** is "beyond qualities and attributes and has no need to accept or reject."

A Hatha Yoga teacher in Ganeshpuri, India, once came to Swami Prakashananda Maharaj and said, "I'm teaching a class of small children from the *Bhagavad Gita*. Could you give me a teaching for them?" We were all waiting for a long teaching from the *Bhagavad Gita*. He replied, "I am nothing, everything is **consciousness**."

What else can be said? To understand this would be enough.

With love,
Your brother, Stephen
(August 12, 1984, Albuquerque, New Mexico)

BIBLIOGRAPHY

BIBLIOGRAPHY

Anandamayi Ma. *Words of Anandamayi Ma.* Varanasi: Shree Anandamayee Charitable Society, 1978.

Bahirzt, B. P. *The Amritanubhava of Jnanadeva.* Bombay: Sirur Press, 1963.

Iyee Bharata. *Selected Stories from Yoga Vasishtha: Elixir of Self Knowledge.*

Jagadiswarananda, Swami. *Devi Mahatm yam.* Sri Ramakrishna Math. Madras: 1978.

Khanna Madhu. *Yantra—The Tantric Symbol of Cosmic Unity.* London: Thames and Hudson Ltd., 1979.

Maharshi Ramana. *Gems from Bhagavan Sri Ramanashram.* Tiruvannamali, 1965.

Maharshi Ramana. *The Spiritual Teaching of Ramana Maharshi.* Boulder and London: Shambhala, 1972.

Maharshi Ramana. *Talks With Sri Ramana Maharshi Ramanashram.* S. India: 1978.

Mookerjee Ajit. *Tantra Asana. A Way to Self-Realization.* Ravi Rumar Basel, Paris, New Delhi, 1971.

Mudallar Devaraja. *Day by Day with Bhagavan.* Tiruvannamali, S. India: Sir Ramanashram, 1977.

Muktananda, Swami. *Play of Consciousness.* Ganeshpun: Shree Gurudev Siddha Peeth Ashram, 1974.

Nikhilananda, Swami. *An Inquiry into the Nature of the Seer and the Seen.* Mysore: Sri Ramakrishna Ashrama, 1976.

Nisargadatta Maharaj. *I Am That,* Durham: Acorn, 1994.

Nisargadatta Maharaj. *Seeds of Consciousness,* Edited by Jean Dunn. Durham: Acorn Press, 1990.

Poddar Hanumanprasad. *The Philosophy of Love.* Rajgangur: Orissa, 1978.

Pradhan, V G. *Jnaneshwari: A Song-Sermon on the Bhagavad Gita, Volumes I and II.* Bombay: Blackie & Sons, 1979.

Rawson, Philip. *The Art of Tantra*. New York and Toronto: Oxford University Press, 1978.

Ramananda Swami. *Tripura Rahasya*. Tiruvannamali, S. India: Sri Ramanashram, 1980.

Singh Jaideva. *Siva Sutra. The Yoga of Supreme Identity*. Delhi, Motilal Banarsidass, 1979.

Singh Jaideva. *Spanda Karikas*. Delhi, Motilal Banarsidass, 1980.

Singh Jaideva. *Vijnana Bhairava or Divine Consciousness*. Delhi, Motilal Banarsidass, 1979.

Wolinsky, Stephen. *Quantum Consciousness*, Bramble Books, 1993